DISCARD

KALAMAZOO LIBRARY SYSTEM

First Catch Your Tiger

Oliver Graham-Jones

First Catch Your Tiger

TAPLINGER PUBLISHING COMPANY | NEW YORK

First published in the United States in 1973 by
TAPLINGER PUBLISHING CO., INC.
New York, New York

Copyright © 1970 by Oliver Graham-Jones
All rights reserved.   Printed in the U.S.A.

No part of this book may be reproduced or transmitted in
any form or by any means, electronic or mechanical, including
photocopy, recording, or any information storage and retrieval
system now known or to be invented, without permission in
writing from the publisher, except by a reviewer who wishes to
quote brief passages in connection with a review written for
inclusion in a magazine, newspaper or broadcast.

Library of Congress Catalog Card Number: 72-8320

ISBN 0-8008-2739-2

To Gilly, the most beautiful and bravest of woman, and to whom, thank God, I am married.

Contents

INTRODUCTION	11
GENESIS	15
1. Whys and Wherefores	17
2. Centaur on the March	31
3. Send It to the Sanny	49
4. Animal Hospital	62
5. Patients Extraordinary	73
6. Tooth and Claw	88
7. When Sabre's Heart Stopped Beating	99
8. Tiger on the Table	110
9. An Elephant Never Forgets	123
10. Creatures Great and Small...	138
11. Unhappy Hippos	152
12. Panda-Monium	164
13. Moon Over Moscow	175
14. To Mate or Not to Mate?	189
15. Zoo-Men's Dilemma	194
16. Extramural Activities	203
EXODUS	219

Illustrations

A blood sample is taken   *between pages* 56-57
Daily Mirror

The toucan's severed lower bill   ”

The artificial lower bill   ”

The bill fitted   ”

A very sedated bear which has rolled into the undergrowth   ”
United Press International

Sabre the puma anaesthetised   ”
Syndication International

Kumari, the tigress, and her cub Suki   *between pages* 136-137
Fox Photos Limited

Kumari on the table   ”
Michael Ward

Kim, the lioness, with Mark at the Zoo   ”
Fox Photos Limited

Diksie: the problem   ”
Fox Photos Limited

The disaster: an attempt is made to raise Diksie   ”
Syndication International

A radiograph of June the llama's leg   ”
Fox Photos Limited

The pins are removed several weeks after the operation   ”
Fox Photos Limited

Fifi and her new mate at Whipsnade   *between pages* 152-153
Syndication International

A dressing is placed on a monkey's injured tail *Fox Photos Limited*	*between pages* 152-153
A baby gorilla after a hernia operation *Granada*	,,
A baby mountain gorilla at the Zoo *Fox Photos Limited*	,,
A budgerigar receives an injection *Feature Photography*	,,
Chi-Chi is introduced to her travelling quarters *Syndication International*	*between pages* 184-185
Chi-Chi meets her pilot and hostess *British European Airways*	,,
With Igor Sosnovski, Director of Moscow Zoo *Novosti Press Agency*	,,
Chi-Chi's Russian quarters	,,
Chi-Chi at London Zoo *Fox Photos Limited*	,,
A final attempt to mate Chi-Chi and An-An *Fox Photos Limited*	,,

Introduction

I have always maintained that the two most dangerous animals to let loose in a zoo unsupervised were a veterinary surgeon and an architect. This is, of course, a very sweeping statement, but basically it is true. The average veterinary surgeon will insist on trying to treat wild animals as though they were domestic stock, and the average architect constructs what might be an architectural poem but it is generally a cage or a building which, while it might be aesthetically satisfying, is generally worse than useless from the point of view of the animal it has to house.

I believe that a successful veterinarian must have that certain flair that makes something more than just a good veterinary surgeon. His patients, after all, cannot tell him how they feel; they can give him precious few guide lines. And so, unless he is a sensitive and intuitive man, his task is made doubly difficult. The immensely long and arduous training that a veterinary surgeon has to undergo gives him a wonderful grounding in animal disease but the one thing it doesn't do, however, is to train him to cope with wild animals, so that if he takes up work in a zoological gardens he is forced to re-think much of his original training and adapt it to these new circumstances. It is only in fairly recent years that zoological collections have thought it worthwhile to have a resident veterinary surgeon on the staff. To me it was obvious that this was an essential part of the running of any zoo. If you simply call the vet. in when an animal is sick you are doubling his difficulties. He does not know the past history of the animal, nor does he know—or can be expected to know—what treatment he can give without harming the animal. But if a veterinary surgeon is resident then he has a continual check on his charges. He can, by experiment, find out which drugs are safe to use and which are not. But most important of all he can, by watching the diet, caging, and day to day treatment of his animals, prevent a great deal of sickness. The advantages of having a resident veterinary officer in any large zoological collection has always been obvious to everyone except those who ran zoos.

During his time with the Zoological Society of London, Oliver Graham-Jones had in his care one of the largest collections of living creatures ever assembled in one spot. It was a formidable undertaking. To have thousands of patients who cannot tell you anything and may be suffering from a bewildering variety of ailments is a job that makes the running of an average hospital pale into insignificance. You will see from this book how Oliver Graham-Jones coped with this herculean task. Altogether it is a fascinating book and shows quite clearly how a zoo veterinarian needs to be a dedicated and knowledgeable man, a man, moreover, of considerable bravery. An infuriated elephant is not, after all, everyone's idea of the ideal patient.

Gerald Durrell
Jersey Wildlife Preservation Trust,
Channel Islands

Genesis

The night sky paled, and tropical birds began to screech their greetings to the dawn. Soon the monkeys would join in with their worried chatter, an elephant would trumpet, and the cacophony of the jungle would prelude my working day.

Sleep-drugged, I switched off the alarm clock, and marvelled, not for the first time, what on earth I had been about in opting for a life where this morning chorus was as much a part of the routine as, say, the clatter of milk bottles on a suburban doorstep.

As I tottered into the flat's bathroom and started to shave, I heard the roar of a lion, compulsively impressive. It was odd to reflect that Camden Town lay less than one mile away!

Over eight hundred mammals of over 250 different species, and here was I, their surgeon and medical adviser. Not for the first time, it seemed a truly daunting prospect, and as startlingly unreal as the environment that had given it birth. How had it all begun, my association with the world's largest living museum, the world's largest collection of wild animals in captivity? Yesterday's sick call had produced a panel of patients that had ranged from the ostrich to the spider-monkey. The day before I had attended a python and, before then, a bear. Just what would be the tally for today?

First Catch Your Tiger

Adjusting my stiffly-starched white coat – the symbol of office – I stepped into the morning air and walked towards the strangest, and sometimes the noisiest, hospital in the world . . . a hospital where the surgeon is often in far greater danger than the patient . . . the hospital where you have to catch your tiger before bringing it to the table . . . the Animal Hospital in London Zoo.

1. Whys and Wherefores

High in the trees at the bottom of our garden, a thrush sang gloriously through the hush of the summer evening. A seven-year-old, lying pensively on his stomach, I turned to my mother, in the deck-chair beside me. 'Why,' I asked her, 'does that little bird sing?'

Mother lowered her knitting, and I could sense her sudden bafflement. 'Why does it sing?' she slowly repeated. 'Well, I don't really know.' Then, brightening, she added, 'Perhaps because it's so happy, dear!'

'But it can't sing *only* when it is feeling happy,' I answered, unimpressed. 'What does it sing about when it's miserable?'

My mother said: 'You *do* ask such very odd questions.'

For the first time in my life I realised that parents were not always all-prescient, the infallible source of information, and the thought really startled me. I wasn't happy until I managed to ferret out the real scientific explanation of the thrush's exquisite vocal powers.

Such was the start of my interest in species other than my own; an interest that stemmed from curiosity, and owed little to sentiment. Today, people often say to me: 'You must always have loved animals,' and look a little shocked when I beg to disagree. Interest in a creature, and the desire to remedy its disabilities, should not be confused with sentimentality; for his patient's sake, the surgeon must always stay uninvolved.

First Catch Your Tiger

I must have been about nine when my mood of inquiry into the behaviour of the living broadened to include reflections on the dead. There was nothing morbid about this, it was just that I wondered *why*.

Why should a field mouse, retrieved with difficulty from the cat, pass away within a minute of its rescue? It bore no signs of injury, it had only been heavily teased, so *why* should it die? My mother said something about a heart attack – 'the fright was too much for it' – but this set me on the path to further questioning. *Why* did the mouse's fright make its heart stop beating? *Why* couldn't its heart be started up again? A clock that had stopped could be wound up, I said. So why could not the mouse's heart? I really must have been a portentous bore!

At the time when all these exercises in natural history-cum-physiology were taking place we were living in a small but very pleasant house on Birmingham's Harborne Estate, built at the turn of the century by a philanthropist of socialistic tendencies who had the rare idea of allotting the houses to honeymoon couples only, in the belief that their offspring, growing up together, would share common interests and develop a strong sense of community. Hating the 'Great Wen', and the murk of the industrial cities, as heartily as Cobbett himself, this estimable character placed much store, and rightly so, on the therapeutic value of the countryside to mind and body, and even in the 'twenties a few minutes' walk would take us into fields and meadows teeming with wild life.

To us children, the place was very special, and even now I can recall the great sense of outrage and personal loss that swept over us when we heard that we were to move from it, and settle elsewhere.

By then there were five of us, and the Harborne Estate

Whys and Wherefores

house had grown too small for the expanding family, but the fact that it was almost bursting at the seams beneath the stress of our explosive energies, or that there was nowhere else in the place where the grown-ups could get a moment's peace, failed to worry us. Extremely content in the home we had known since birth the threat to remove us from our cocoon, with all the security it represented, filled us with terror.

However, when the dread day arrived, we found that things weren't so bad after all. Our new quarters, only half a mile from World's End Lane – nowadays engulfed by the concrete ocean of development – offered us even greater scope than 8 Park Edge for following rural activities. What with our encounters with the cattle – grazing in lush fields where today not a single blade of grass can be seen – our fishing for tiddlers in the nearby stream, and our long walks with Father (a beloved man) through the meadows and the woods, we lived the life of country children, and enjoyed it, and my interest in animals grew into an absorbing one. In fact, it was at 15 Milford Road, Harborne, that I had my first 'veterinary' experience – treating my dog for injuries sustained in heroic battle.

Our dog was a mongrel Irish terrier, with a nervous, sensitive nose, and soft brown eyes that impressed all who saw him with his gentleness. Unfortunately perhaps for him, his looks belied his nature.

Pat was a battler, a sort of canine d'Artagnan; a swaggering, carefree blade with courage and style. Impulsive in his temperament, the only fault in his fighting was that invariably he would pick for his opponent a dog with a weight and size that was double that of his own. It seemed almost a point of honour with him, this nice discrimination,

19

and he bore with equanimity the inevitable consequences, painful though they must have been.

So, when we moved to Milford Road it was no surprise that he should fix on the biggest dog in the village in his challenge to assert his (far-reaching) claims of domain. Nor that, undeterred by honourable scars, he should return to the attack the following day, and then attack again a couple of days after that, a process that became repetitive, and was deplored by everyone in the family except me, Pat's titular master. *I* thought him stupendous.

Twice or thrice a week, our dog would be engaged with his rival, contesting with him for mastery and always getting the worst of it: and each time he would return home extremely late, as if anxious not to disturb my parents; but to let the sun go down upon their well-merited wrath. On such occasions, as he seemed to expect, I would creep downstairs in my pyjamas to let him quietly into the kitchen, and bathe and cleanse his wounds as best I knew. Yet, every time, he would prevent the true worth of the 'treatment' being accurately assessed, for long before his injuries had a chance to heal, he would be off for the next round, 'to fight and fight again!'

Eventually, however, our mutual conspiracy of silence failed to work, Pat's fights became such a scandal, and caused such public complaint. He wrecked the local paper shop one final morning by choosing to fight indoors his pet aversion while the commuters tried to catch their bus. After that my parents presented him to the postman!

Although it caused me much heartache at the time, I can scarcely blame them for making their decision. But the memory of the sense of companionship – or was it patronage? – that I experienced in those clandestine meetings was to stay with me for many years, and not be duplicated in my

Whys and Wherefores

dealings with wild animals. When sick or hurt, the domestic pet must rely upon man for help, because he is imprinted with man's image and dependent upon him: but one of the first lessons I was to learn in my career at the zoo was that the wild animal is exactly the opposite to the domestic in his reactions to pain and sickness. Shunning the society even of his own, and ready to resist with all his force any man-made effort to treat him, the wild animal is a loner. Subject only to the direction of his savage whims and actions, he is his own worst enemy, and his 'doctor's' too.

Yet even the wildest creature – when in captivity – has the occasional, very tenuous link with man. It is one that is likely to snap at the first symptom of stress, and one where the initiative comes from the keeper, rather than the captive 'kept'. But it *is* a link, and one can only try to develop it.

A few years ago, when reviewing the dietary of the animal population of London Zoo, I made the astonishing discovery that the keepers were using no fewer than forty types of dog biscuit. Forty! – I had never before realised that there were so many brands in the world, let alone in the Zoological Gardens!

On analysis, however, I found the difference of type to be more apparent than real, and in some cases existing only in the colour of the container and the name on the label; even though their variations of price and shape must have provided a nightmare for book-keepers.

When I had recovered from my surprise, my first impulse was to standardise the lot, and give one brand only my official blessing, but this was an idea that I later felt obliged to modify.

The variety of (apparent) choices made by the keepers reflected in a sense their close relationship with their animals. They liked to 'shop around' and get their individual

First Catch Your Tiger

charges something special – something that was 'different' from the fare doled out to others. Would I – should I – risk offending these devoted men, the very backbone of the Zoo's administration, by insisting that I knew better than they as regards what would suit their favourites?

In the end, I did succeed in pressing on them a standard biscuit – designed by Graham-Jones, and of good nutritional value – but only when I had allowed each keeper to take ten per cent of his previous 'special' brand. Then, and only then, were tempers mollified, and general concern abated. Once more, morale soared high.

By that time, I had realised what at first I had overlooked: namely that to bar the keepers from exerting any sort of choice would substantially weaken their personal links with the animals, and thus might well do more damage than any amount of added vitamin-value, or economies in expenditure could repair. The keepers would feel that their individual responsibility for their animals had been lessened, and something precious would have been lost in the process.

An exaggeration? Even as a child, I had experienced the sort of special interest, and understanding, that comes from having a pet exclusively under one's own control and care.

I had been permitted to keep a pet rabbit, a plump little female called Binkie, who was housed in a hutch outside the kitchen door. It was a roomy hutch and, by all standards appertaining to the accommodation of rabbits, a comfortable hutch as well; but this did not prevent me from developing an acute anxiety for the health of its inmate – an anxiety that arose from a somewhat original concept of something I'd heard called New-Monia.

This dread disease, I gathered, was a real killer, and

Whys and Wherefores

people became its victims as the result of catching cold. So what about Binkie? With her home exposed to every wind that blew, Binkie, I reasoned, was at very real risk, and my feelings were outraged by the fact that the rest of our family did not seem to share my perspicacity, and consequent apprehension.

This fear for the rabbit's well-being did not wane with the passage of time, indeed it increased, and increased to such an extent that, as had happened during the regime of our dog, I found myself involved in nocturnal expeditions to make sure that she was 'all right', and protect her, as far as I could, from the thing that menaced her.

By late autumn I had become involved in providing Binkie with such aids to resistance against the weather as a hot water bottle, strips of blanket etc., and inevitably my activities had become a domestic talking-point. Equally inevitably, my parents then imposed a ban!

While encouraging us children to have a due regard for the health of our pets, and always emphasising our responsibility for their general well-being, my parents felt that my practice was carrying principle to extremes. After all, small boys have been known to catch cold too! But I received their edict extremely ungraciously, and failed completely to understand their natural concern.

The climax of my involvement came about when Binkie gave birth to a litter, which Mother, unable to find adopters, had destroyed. This caused me so to fret myself about the rabbit's feelings – its sense of loss at being deprived of its children, and so forth – that I developed a psychological stress, and my parents, to spare me much painful conflict, eventually had the animal 'put down'!

Such was my first experience, although in microcosm, of the hard decision-making that can confront one in situations where an animal's existence is considered to be likely to clash with the interests and security of man. Even today the memory of it hurts.

And yet, of course, my parents' action had a logic about it that contrasted very favourably with the sort of feckless sentimentalism that so often is part of the stock in trade of the 'animal-lover'. Once having decided – although wrongly, I feel – that the health of one of their progeny was in danger, they reverted to an instinct as old as nature itself; the instinct to preserve one's species, in the battle for survival. However, I can't pretend that this philosophy was of much comfort to me at the time!

Curiosity about why a wild bird should sing . . . dramatisation over the plight of a rabbit, whose sentiments I equated with those of man . . . sympathy and comradeship for my embattled dog . . . it would be wrong to say that any single one of these factors was decisive in my choice of a career. Nor was there any individual revelation that caused me to tell myself, 'I am going to be a vet!' The process contrived to grow on me, with me hardly noticing it.

At grammar school, my interests in animals and their habits acquired for me a certain fame, or notoriety, that reached its peak when I made a 'home' for white mice in my jacket pocket, and Mother discovered their droppings. For the sake of my pets' personal safety I then made the hurried decision to take them with me to school, where I was able to provide them with a far roomier place to nest – inside the back of my desk.

For a while, this arrangement worked out famously, but the hour of reckoning came when the master happened to ask me to produce an exercise book. I delved into the desk, fumbled in the back of it, and then felt my face go oven-hot with embarrassment. All that remained of the book I now unwillingly presented was a mass of soggy paper, pulped and perforated by a thousand bites.

The master had reached my side before I could even drop the desk lid, and there, exposed to his startled gaze – and as was to be shown, his abrasive wit – were my original white mice and more – breeding like mad things, and with healthy appetites too!

This incident marked the conclusion of my social study of the domesticated mouse. Feeling that the situation had got slightly out of hand, I agreed to get rid of them, and swapped them at the exchange rate of one full bodied mouse for two marbles, a baby mouse for one.

*

Although the white-mouse affair could be said to have shown me that the care of animals could sometimes prove to be of commercial advantage, I don't think it had much relevance to my future.

A few years ago at the Zoo, when faced with the problem of how to anaesthetise gorillas, we produced a giant gas box which we placed flush up against the opening in the animal's den in the hope that the gorilla would wander into it.

But the gorilla is a cunning and highly suspicious customer, and does not lightly forsake the security of its familiar environment – much persuasion is needed before it will play the game according to your rules. So, by way of inducement, we placed a full-length mirror at the far end of the box. Immediately the animal saw himself reflected there, his wariness vanished and he responded the way we wanted. As he went into the box, the slide fell shut behind him, sealing him off for the inflow of the gas. He had been trapped by his own curiosity.

First Catch Your Tiger

It was probably this self-same quality – curiosity – that played the major part in deciding me when still a fourth former as to what path *I* should take in the years ahead. Curiosity, and a perverse desire to swim against the tide. For my decision was not likely to be enthusiastically received.

My brother was training as a doctor, my sister was training as a teacher, and Mama had a single-minded idea – inspired by I know not what – that I should be a dental surgeon: indeed she had entered my name for the Dental College long before academically speaking I had cut my own teeth, let alone had nourished any ambitions about operating on anyone else's.

Neither were my schoolmasters particularly keen on my idea of following a veterinary career. Indeed, when I started to inquire about how to set about it, I found that it was a mystery not only to me, but to adults as well.

This became particularly obvious when I was one day sent for by the headmaster. A bit of a character, as they say, and an authoritarian of godlike dimensions, one of his characteristically brilliant ideas had been to install traffic lights outside his study door. You took a place in the queue, but when your turn arrived, you didn't just knock and walk in. You waited until the lights changed to amber!

Unfortunately, I was so hypnotised by this device, and so put-out to find it apparently fixed at a baleful red, that I did not move fast enough when the signal changed, and had literally to be dragged inside the study.

However, after this ominous beginning, it transpired that the appointment had been fixed for no sinister purpose: the Head had merely wanted to see what ideas I had regarding my career. This was a standard routine of his when boys reached their early teens, and very efficient he was in advising them on how to pursue their choice. The Army, the Civil Service, yes, even the Ministry, he knew just how his pupils could best get there.

But when, my conscience at rest, I told the Headmaster that I wished to be a veterinary officer his air of paternal assurance swiftly vanished. A 'vet'? Why a vet? Wasn't I entering the dental profession? I explained my views and repeated my request. Could he tell me, please, what would I need to qualify? Did he know where I should write? Eventually the interview terminated with me no wiser than before, and the Head quite foxed and a little irritated at being, for once, left without an answer.

I left the Headmaster's presence with the moral clear in my mind that if you wanted to find out anything worthwhile, you had better do it yourself. But it was only after I had pestered the most unlikely sources for information that I finally tackled the only people who really knew about it – the Royal College of Veterinary Surgeons. And no sooner had I learned what I wanted to know – and obtained, after some discussion, an unenthused parental blessing, than I almost changed my mind and shelved the idea altogether. Paradoxically, it was my father who put me back on course . . .

My father, a journeyman silversmith by articles, who had suffered severely during the depression, had started up in business as a shipfitter using plastics, and was doing remarkably well. At the end of each ocean-crossing there were calls made on his services, from ships whose names today have an almost legendary fame – the *Queen Mary* and the *Queen Elizabeth* among them – and so brisk was the business that I was enlisted as part-time worker, during the school holidays.

First Catch Your Tiger

Of course all this activity with its introduction to the big liners seemed highly dramatic to one of my impressionable age. It was certainly lucrative when compared with my normal pocket money allowance, and required no undue concentration. My studies began to suffer, and I toyed with the idea of becoming a shipfitter too – until Father, sensing it, put an end to it. Calling me into his office, he said, 'You come into this business only over my dead body!'

Father had seen how a man without qualifications except his intelligence and capacity to work could have his livelihood threatened, and then removed, by market pressures over which he exerted no control. He was determined that his son should not be similarly vulnerable, but should have what he had lacked, the equivalent of a university course in a specialised profession. So back I went, to pursue my real ambitions.

Having overcome her initial incredulity at my failure to be enthused by dentistry, my mother was a tower of strength during the months that followed.

She fixed an interview for me at the Royal Veterinary College – to decide whether or not I might enrol as a student – and then, as ready to fight for my career as she had hitherto been to oppose it, she journeyed to London with me, to give me moral support.

Unfortunately, I did not know that she was feeling ill . . .

It was just as the train pulled into Paddington that Mother collapsed. I had never before encountered such a thoroughly frightening event. Terror-stricken, I ran to the nearby hospital, only to be brusquely told by someone who probably did not understand the urgency, 'We have no ambulance available. You must bring her in yourself!'

A country bumpkin, as far as London taxis were concerned, I was quite uncertain as to what they would charge, or whether I had sufficient for the fare. Nor, oddly enough, did it occur to me to open my mother's handbag, or explain the situation to sympathetic bystanders. Instead, I lifted her in my arms, and carried her to the casualty department!

There, they told me to leave her and call back after my interview – which she insisted I must keep – but when I returned, I found she had contracted the same illness I had once imagined threatening Binkie. My mother had pneumonia!

In view of my prejudices in respect of this disease, the effect the news had upon me can well be imagined. It seemed as if the world was coming to an end. And yet there was my mother, obstinately refusing to listen to the doctors, and insisting, in face of all protests, that she leave for home! I was horrified at the thought of her taking such a risk – yet equally horrified at the thought of leaving her. Beset by the medical warnings, and with my mind completely confused, it says much for my awe of Mother that I finally signed her out, and escorted her back to Birmingham in a lather of fear and grief.

As soon as we reached New Street Station, I did what I had not dared to do in London: I ordered a cab. 'Go like hell', I grandly ordered the aged driver. 'And don't stop for the lights!'

Quite suddenly I had changed from boy to man.

Well, Mother survived her illness, and even though my father was so upset that it was at least a week before he would even listen to my – understandably muddled –

First Catch Your Tiger

account of the interview, from that moment on my path in life was pretty firmly established.

I entered the Royal Veterinary College in September 1936 and there, at the focus-point of my ambitions, so to speak, I found myself prey to the most awful homesickness, and the most shaming doubts about my own ability.

2. Centaur on the March

A place with the gloss, and much of the tang, of new white paint . . . a place of austerity, coldly gleaming in wan sunshine and with windows whose glassy stare seemed to cover every inch of the trim and weedless drive . . . such was my first impression of the institution in which, for better or worse, I had been assigned for the next five years of my young life: the Royal Veterinary College.

Standing in its own enclave with an air of clinical detachment, it seemed as divorced from the smokes and smells of Camden Town as a Western consular building from the lives of the coolies of pre-war Shanghai.

Like other new boys for many years before me, I found that the first human who condescended to speak to me in this aloof environment was Sibley the porter – six-foot-four in height, and straight-backed as a soldier which, indeed, was what he had been. In his carefully pressed and stiffly brushed livery, its darkness relieved only by a bank of medal ribbons, Sibley made a most formidable figure, and the 'Sir' with which he greeted you was both paternal and sardonic. Here you felt – and rightly so – was a man who had no illusions about students or their importance: he had seen so many of them come and go that he was past any sentiment for the species, save, perhaps, a certain pity.

In the face of this most admirable of custodians, my explanation of who I was, and my requests as to where I should go, turned into a series of stammering inadequacies received with civil condescension. Sibley, who knew it all, deigned to explain it all – and then left me on my own, and acutely conscious of it.

No longer a boy at school, to be organised, and told precisely what to do, I would have to make my own way, and under my own steam. The world of the R.V.C. was far too busy to stand still while a not yet seventeen-year-old attempted to get into its orbit, and the implications of this were clear to me from the moment of my arrival. Here I would have the choice – the man's choice – of work or idleness. I would be offered the facilities for study, I would be introduced to a curriculum that was staggeringly comprehensive. But no one would insist on the path I chose to follow and the consequence of any sins of omission would fall on my own head.

The prospect was somewhat daunting.

Founded in the late 18th century, the Royal Veterinary College was undergoing a comprehensive rebuilding programme when I started there, and its decor was severely contemporary in the 'hygienic', if rather sterile, fashion of the 'thirties.

Even the canteen, a gleaming mass of stainless steel, was in a chaste sort of way a thing of beauty, and like most of the other new buildings was built on such a scale that 'vast' was the operative term when one's only yardstick was the remembered scene at school. The canteen could cater for 350 students at a sitting, and they descended on it like a pack of hungry wolves. But the most visually impressive of all the spectacles the College had to offer was its magnificent dissecting theatre, appearing to be as large as an aircraft hangar.

From the trestles a large number of animals – and parts of

animals – hung from chains, to be lowered or heightened for examination by the students. Exhibits included a comprehensive range of specimens, and dominating the scene was a very dead horse, pickled and ready for dissection. I regarded this with the sickness of despair, eyes streaming from the acrid fumes of formalin.

Comparing notes with my contemporaries about those early days at the College, it is clear to me that my initial attitude, of abject defeatism, was by no means unique. Others too fell prey to the disease, but feigned indifference.

The programme was extremely comprehensive, and we were awed by all the things we would have to know. In some cases it was even more advanced than that judged appropriate for human medicine, for one would have to diagnose cases without recourse to the information a human patient could have supplied. Animal Husbandry, Anatomy, Physiology, Pharmacology, Pathology, Medicine, Surgery – all these subjects, and more, had to be assimilated during the five years of one's labours, and there were major examinations at annual intervals, which culminated in the fateful finals, taken in my case while still twenty-one.

The lecturers were men of great talent, and several of them were 'characters' as well. We discussed their eccentricities with juvenile levity, but we discussed them behind their backs, and completely without malice. In actual fact, we regarded them with little short of awe.

One of the greatest of professors to bestride the teaching scene affected the morning suit style – frock coat and striped trousers – that had been favoured by *his* tutor and, probably, his tutor's tutor before him. With a fresh rose in his lapel, inches below the rim of his severely glossed winged collar, his sole concession to modern trends was in his phrenetic chain-smoking. 'Wearing' (it's the only word for it!) a succession of cigarettes beneath his bushy ('Wicked Squire' type) moustache, and replacing each one only when it had burned down to the butt and had started to singe his lips, he would hold the class mesmerised – waiting for his imminent conflagration. The major points of his discourse were emphasised by a finger adorned by a monstrous ring, and nicotine. Yet, appearances notwithstanding, he was a truly splendid teacher, of international repute, and had written what was then the only encyclopaedia of veterinary medicine. He was also a highly competent practitioner, and also demonstrator of the use of the surgeon's knife if required.

It was under the regime of the late Professor McCunn that I received my first impression of what was *really* entailed by veterinary surgery – entailed in flesh and blood as distinct from print and theory. This baptism of fire came just after my arrival.

In the grounds of the College was and still exists 'The Ride' – a covered way in which horse patients could be exercised. It had a tan surface that was primarily designed for the benefit of the lame, but also served other purposes, somewhat more grisly.

Seeing a crowd gathered on its fringes one morning, I approached the scene to observe a faintish smoke arising from its centre. Momentarily, I thought that someone had perhaps lit a small fire, and then, as heads parted, I saw the Professor of Anatomy.

The steam was rising from what he was holding in his hand; something large and white and bloody that he had cut from the belly of the horse that lay at his feet.

I took another look. And observed the 'thing' was a testicle! He was lifting it to display it to his students, and he was doing so with the part nonchalant, part triumphant, expression of a conjuror who having succeeded in dazzling his audience with expertise awaits their applause. I experienced a shuddering sense of revulsion at the sight, but it did not last for long. And afterwards, even the pickled horse in the theatre held no horrors for me.

The Professor certainly had an enthusiasm for his calling – so much so that some of it even rubbed off on his audiences, a factor which said quite a lot for his 'style' for he was dealing with some fairly unlikely pupils.

Forming a very sharp contrast to the main buildings of the College were the older properties in the grounds, and the 'country' smell of the stables, and the odour of burning in the blacksmith's shop, where we learned to shoe horses. I for one found these reminders of the outdoor life to be were oddly comforting. I still possess 'my' shoe, mounted now as a desk clock.

In the 'thirties it was fashionable to be a veterinary surgeon. All the terribly nice people – the socially acceptable people – had their large country houses, their horses and dogs, their shooting and fishing. True that the traditional pastimes of retirement on the ancestral estates or service in the Army had given place to the Stock Exchange in the choice of an elder son's career, but for the brighter type of the younger sons of the 'County' a veterinary career seemed the natural thing to turn to. For the duller ones there was still the Church!

It might be that today these fellows might grate on the nerves of their less pecunious colleagues. With their confidence founded on wallets twice as thick as their heavy tweed sports-jackets they might well give rise to envious reflections, or, perhaps more likely, would themselves assume the leadership of the 'underprivileged', believing that any new hierarchy should still be topped by the Upper Crust. At the time, however, these men of substance and property merely served to fascinate the rest of us; even though there might be reflections on their lack of 'dedication'.

The racing set was strong, and so was their 'larking' – and beneath their sparkling, affluent tutelage, I began to develop a taste for London life that at times seemed extreme to my long-suffering parents, and included certain aspects that are better by far forgotten. And yet, it is best not to exaggerate my colleagues' influence on my switch towards the Bright Lights if not the Turf: the main cause was apprehension. I was becoming convinced that I could not absorb the College's formidable agenda, and at seventeen the five years' study needed under the old regulations to qualify seemed to stretch into eternity. Senior students of the College, distinguished by their white coats, and their stethoscopes with which they adorned themselves, seemed *so* senior as to be almost elder statesmen. In short, I was ill-equipped to deal with the challenge posed by the College's emphasis on freedom of choice for its students and studies suffered accordingly.

The dangers of the comfortable rut into which I had so gracefully been content to sink, were first brought home to me by the Delphic Mr Sibley.

Confronting me one morning as I returned belatedly to College – no doubt after a late breakfast – he stood in my path and said:

'Mr Jones, *Sir*,' (and never had that 'Sir' sounded more unlikely!) 'you are about to be expelled from the College!'

It was as if he had emptied a bucket of water over me, I

regarded him with incredulous astonishment. '*Expelled!* Just what have I done?'

'Mr Jones, sir,' he said. 'You have not paid your fees!'

It turned out that I had not paid certain fees to the examining body – even though the need to do so had been advertised on the notice-board. 'And this you have evidently not read, sir,' said Sibley severely. 'You have not bothered to read it!'

Well, of course, back at school, they'd have told us, reminded us, asked us to learn the contents of the wretched notice by heart, or else write down, five hundred times, something along the lines, 'I must not forget etc. . . .' But it was useless, as I realised, to complain that the R.V.C. should have done so. At the College we were considered to be adults, with the responsibility for looking after ourselves that the status required. Feebly I ventured to ask if all hope had died for me.

It transpired that there was only one thing I could do – get my fee, and take it to the Royal College of Veterinary Surgeons, and there eat humble pie, confess my sins, and throw myself on their mercy, so this I did.

I emerged from the solemn conclave that eventually announced my reprieve with the resolution that never again would I neglect to study the notice board.

The next jolt to my contentment with our fashionable high junketing came at the end of the year, when we sat the annual examinations. I failed Anatomy, and failed miserably, and was faced by the need to break the news to my parents.

Before I left for college, Father had insisted that I wrote home regularly and had emphasised the point with the expressive phrase 'No letter means No money.' At the time, it had sounded a civilised exchange, but on this occasion I felt that it would be better to give him in person my version of events: the stark facts on paper might even aggravate his anticipated annoyance.

Father had recently made an additional stipulation, that whenever I decided to come home for the weekend I must first ring him to give my estimated time of arrival. This was because I had invested all my savings – £18 – in a dilapidated old Austin 7 car that kept my mother fretting herself about my precious safety. With things as they were, however, a phone-call might prove to be an embarrassment – I didn't want parental questions about my examination luck to flow furiously over the telephone lines and I was careful to keep news of my coming very brief and delivered it at a time when Father was out. This done, I embarked on the journey in a mood of sheer depression, and with strong forebodings that the worst was still to come.

This presentiment was justified. I was involved in a collision with a runaway vehicle, and the car was almost wrecked. It just wasn't my day.

Until then, I'd laughed at my mother's fears, but that homeward drive provided a brutal corrective. The door of the car was ripped off; the chassis battered and bent. I emerged from the debris shocked and shaken, and with head and hands running in blood. However, I was lucky not to have been more seriously injured, and eventually, after much effort, the car was got to work.

Against all advice I then decided to press on. I didn't want to alarm my parents with long-distance calls, which might only serve to exaggerate the matter. Again, I had begun to feel that in view of the vexing nature of my news the sorry spectacle the car and I presented might even be a blessing in disguise. It might conceivably soften-up Father!

Our house stood at the top of a hill and it was Father's

custom to stand there waiting my arrival. Today was no exception to the rule, and I noticed with sinking heart that he was looking at his watch. My wounds were bleeding again, and I was in very bad order indeed, but as I brought the old banger to a clattering halt, not one word of sympathy did my parent bestow. 'You are over an hour late,' he commented bleakly, 'and I am informed that you have failed your examinations!'

I started to bleat something expressive of my regrets, but he waved me to silence. 'I will see you in my study – when you have cleaned yourself up.'

It was a difficult interview, the one that followed this unpromising introduction, and what made it even harder was the fact that I knew my father's annoyance to be thoroughly justified. I had failed through my own fault, and no one else's. I had failed not through lack of capacity but through a mixture of self-doubt and self-indulgence. Say that he should decide that I wasn't worth his sacrifice? Say that he should decide to withdraw me from the College?

Oddly enough, it was then – and only then – that I realised to the full how much I would miss the place, and how I had imperilled the substance for the shadow.

However, the session ended on a far better note than I had expected, and there was no suggestion that my studies should come to an end. Instead, I was abjured to 'make a go of it' and this I most sincerely resolved to do.

At the conclusion of our review, my father permitted himself a rare smile. 'Well now,' he said, 'we'll talk over a glass of sherry, and I will allow you to tell me what you have done to your car!'

*

This lesson learned, I continued my progress through

College in reasonably studious style, and with no incident to make it really noteworthy, or even particularly noticeable.

Our work-routine was strenuous, but livened by the usual student horseplay, and the occasion when we raided our rivals at King's College, and 'castrated' with hammer and chisel, Reggie, their cherished metal lion, was probably the major highlight of the period. The inter-collegiate rugby matches were also to leave their memories, and their scars. 'If you can't beat 'em – kill 'em,' was our slogan.

I am often surprised by the way in which the student is nowadays regarded as some sort of social phenomenon, as if there's been nothing like him ever before. In fairness to the student, I must record that this is very far from the truth.

The contemporary student is said to be obsessed with chasing sex. Incredibly, we too were so afflicted – and I find nothing novel in the news that young males fancy themselves as seducers. It has happened before.

And yet, one has to admit it, there *were* differences between the practices of us students of the 'thirties and those prevalent today. Differences of degree.

Formerly, a successful seduction was a private affair – something confined to you and the young woman concerned. Bragging about it was considered to be 'not quite the thing' or (far worse!) was dismissed as 'adolescent'. Today the trend is to give one's sexual prowess the maximum publicity, with scant concern for the girl on whom one has proved it. Again, one persevered in a seduction only when the other party appeared to be 'willing'. Today, the girl who chooses to say 'No' is bitterly denounced as someone a bit frigid, or even 'queer'. My generation would not have considered this riposte to a brush-off as very clever.

Similar moral reflections come to mind when recalling

our student 'rags'. Sometimes these were more lively – and more vulgar – than the 'demos' that are currently the rage: but we did observe a certain code of conduct, and assumed responsibility for our actions.

In no circumstances were members of the public to be involved in our mutual hell-raising. In no circumstances was serious injury to be done. Reprisals between colleges were conducted on a territorial basis and were never personal in the sense that they were directed at individual members. Damage was made good from a common fund. There were no manifestations of 'Student Power' and the like, and our rioting never assumed an ugly political flavour. We might pinch a P.C.'s helmet, we'd never kick him in the groin!

However, on the whole our activities were no more dissimilar to those of our current counterparts than those of adults in the 'thirties when compared with those of today. Each age sets its own particular trend and fashion: people remain very much the same.

In my time, the done thing for the modish student, after a night Up West, was to take his breakfast in tails, with a carnation in his buttonhole. In the era of today's permissive society, it's considered to be 'with it' if you take a sleeping bag into Trafalgar Square.

We had some very serious students in the years before the war, we had the gilded sons of idleness as well. Today, the latter are definitely less 'gilded' and we call them 'long-haired layabouts' instead. But the 'serious' are so very, very serious that one sometimes feels they should take courses on how to laugh.

In fact, the really new – and very disturbing – feature of the prevailing scene is the part that drugs have come to play in it.

First Catch Your Tiger

One can grow out of the ritual of fifteen pints on a Saturday night – just as one grows out of the hearty rugger that inspired it. But, once addicted, only a minute handful can hope to escape the killing grasp of narcotics.

*

In 1939, the outbreak of war brought to a halt the stately minuet of donnish politics, and scattered us – Oxford Grouper and Rugby Blue alike – into the English countryside. For the Royal Veterinary College, evacuation entailed a removal to the delightful Berkshire village of Streatley, where we spent the next few months before embarking on our finals. To my astonishment, I qualified at the very first attempt.

Flushed with the arrogance of youth that I now find so perplexing when encountered among the young people of today, I immediately abandoned all ideas of becoming assistant to an established veterinary surgeon, and purchased myself the nucleus of a practice. And then, in what may now appear to have been a rather quaint example of second-thoughts, I volunteered for the Army, and the Army said No.

The Italian campaign was about to begin, and the need was for mules, for transport work in the mountains. The Army, until then understandably preoccupied with armoured warfare, had to find men who could handle animals, and advertised in the newspapers for them. But when I applied I was told that there were obstacles in the way. I was a married man, in a reserved occupation: more important still, I happened to own a practice. My job was to keep animals fit for the battle of the land.

Several weeks went by before the Army relented, and

Centaur on the March

then only because of my persistent pressure. By that time I had got rid of the major difficulty by putting my assistant – we had been students together – in charge of the concern, and Whitehall was probably sick of the sight of my face, and the sound of my wearisome opportuning. I found myself in Italy in next to no time at all.

From the snug expanding practice in the pleasantest part of Surrey, to the Field Remount Station on the circuitous road to Rome . . . from sitting up with a sick cow in the calm of an English meadow, to supplying teams of mules . . . the transition was sharp, and very far from pleasant. And yet, like so many others of my age-group, I don't think I would have liked to have missed my share of the mutual misery. I hated the life, but the experience made it worth while.

I danced with the local mayor's daughter, and saw the fleas dance with us – in her hair. I impounded sheep to feed the officers' mess; and was forced to pay for my cheek by an irate Town Mayor. I slept in war-blasted ruins, waking to dust the snow off my sleeping bag, and curse the 'Sunny South' as a criminal fraud. And then an old enemy caught up with me: Brucellosis.

Causing excessive aborting among cattle, and severe illness with prolonged febrile attacks in man, brucellosis sometimes takes fifteen years or more to run itself out: certainly it took all that time for it to run out on me.

I had contracted the disease without knowing it, back in England as a student, where I had handled infected cows. It first manifested itself in a temperature that rose to danger point, and a series of excruciating headaches. It resulted in being sent out of the line for diagnosis.

After a Cook's tour of American hospitals – the food and hospitality were marvellous! – and one less well endowed,

First Catch Your Tiger

but efficient British counterpart, I found myself being invalided home, 'Y' listed for discharge.

Although my departure from the Army should have appeared to me as a gift from Heaven, I didn't see it in that light; not at the time. Unexpectedly, I became quite upset about it, and was for a while almost rudderless. I missed my friends and the comradeship that, despite our unspeakable cynicism about a soldier's calling, was no empty word, but a very strong bond indeed. As a survivor, I knew that I was 'one of the lucky ones', but like other survivors I was almost ashamed of my luck. Man is never really content – it takes an animal to be that!

It was perhaps because of this – a sense of guilt maybe at the contrast between my fate and that of others – that I began to have serious doubts about my civilian career. The practice was booming, but was this all I really wanted? Was it just a fat bank balance that I had been aiming at, when first I'd wondered what caused a thrush to sing? Was I *really* helping animals? Or was I merely cashing in on them, by enhancing their productivity for the farmer? Discontentedly I began to look on 'profit' as a dirty word; and vicariously condemned it. By then I was rich enough to be able to afford to do so.

It was in 1947 that I found a panacea for my doubts; by deciding to invest part of the proceeds from the practice in a line that, at that time, was almost completely untried. I decided to finance and design an animal hospital.

One of the first of its kind outside the teaching schools, I wanted to offer a first-class veterinary service, provided with up-to-date facilities for diagnosis and surgery: facilities that, otherwise, owners could not afford. By the time I had completed the place it had cost me all my savings and more.

It took five years for disillusionment to set in; not disillusionment with the product, but with the way people treated it.

In the main, prosperous farmers seemed to regard their animals with as little affection, or sense of responsibility, as a mill-owner would concede to a piece of machinery: once it ceased to be economic you threw it on the scrap-heap! Faced with the cost of saving an animal, with few exceptions they would opt for the bullet rather than the syringe.

Problems too were posed by those of the private pet-owners, who hopelessly over-indulged their expensive pekes and pooches and then, hypochondriacs by proxy, as it were, spent their time wondering what was wrong with the dogs' health. These people were very wasteful of one's time and patience; the hospital had been built for far more serious purposes.

The fact that the project was situated in the heart of a garrison area also proved to be a not unmixed blessing. Soldiers were perpetually acquiring pets, and bringing them in for treatment. But they were also perpetually discarding pets as they themselves moved on from one base to another. In most cases they would seek to find a home for the animal, placing it with one of their successors: but in others they merely 'lost' them, leaving them to fend for themselves. I once found myself feeding and housing twenty-eight dogs abandoned by these men. The work entailed in finding new owners occupied weeks.

As time went by, it became abundantly clear to me that the practice of any of the more enlightened veterinary skills was in the ultimate dependent on the depths of the owner's pocket: or rather on his willingness to dig therein, which is not always the same thing.

While not hesitating to act ruthlessly when the occasion

demands it – when the health of an animal is so bad that nothing else can terminate its misery – I have always hated the job of executioner. And the build-up of friction that was created by the frequent requests I got to put an animal 'down' when it was perfectly unnecessary to do so reached its peak in 1950.

Disappointed, and somewhat bitter, I decided to close the hospital and dispose of the practice, too.

I had had enough, and more, of the dilemma where there was no choice between destroying an animal, or else footing the bill oneself – and we very often did – for taking the trouble to find it a new home.

In a revulsion of feeling, I decided to quit veterinary work altogether and enter my name for one of London's famous medical schools. From now on, I would switch to human medicine, and try to qualify as a doctor.

As far as I'm aware, the doctor never shoots the patient.

*

The medical profession appeared to have no problem over recruiting. The medical schools had long waiting-lists of volunteers. I soon realised that it would be twelve months or more before I could gain admission to the one I had specially selected, and that in the meanwhile I must do something about getting a job.

This problem was resolved by my taking an appointment in the Anatomy Department of the Royal Veterinary College. It was a junior post, but I didn't really care. All that I wanted was a means of maintaining myself while I waited for the opening of the medical course. I was resolved that never again would I involve myself in the purely veterinary routines.

On the positive side, I looked forward very much to the

rewarding task of bettering the lot of patients who were of one's own species, and whose feelings and reactions were similar to one's own. Again, in human medicine you were able to draw on the National Health Service in order to treat patients who could not otherwise afford the drugs required. In animal medicine this just did not apply.

No, I decided, I was through with being a 'vet' – but this resolution was easier to make than to maintain in practice.

At the College was a professor who remembered me as a student, when he had done his best to encourage me in such skills as I possessed, and was genuinely concerned at my leaving the profession. One day, taking me aside, he told me that, owing to various changes in the laws relating to veterinary surgeons and animal care the Zoo had decided to look for a resident veterinary officer. Why didn't I put in my name for the post? While appreciating his kindness I told him I wasn't interested; but my friend was not one to abandon lightly a position. Refusing to take my 'No' as final he tried again, and then repeated his efforts, until finally, really to humour him I agreed to attend an interview. I was confident that the job would not be offered me for until then my veterinary experience had been confined to agricultural animals and pets. I knew as much about wild animals as most of my contemporaries, and that 'much' was very little.

Thus when the day of the interview arrived, I entered the room nonchalantly, not giving a damn, and confident that the procedure would be over in a matter of minutes. Two and a half hours passed before I emerged, much humbled and cut down to size.

The questions put to me by the serious men before whom I had paraded my ignorance of wild life had revealed that that ignorance was even more abysmal than I had imagined it to be. And oddly enough, they had also touched off a grudging curiosity on my part regarding the nature of the job, in which, until then, I had been disinterested.

How did one administer medicine to a tiger? How could a tiger be brought to the operating table? Come to think of it, how did one diagnose the illness of a tiger?

The more I dwelt on such problems of treatment, the more did I begin to feel a certain regret that for me they must always remain purely academic. I found myself admitting that the job *had* presented a challenge, and *could* have been interesting, had they asked me to accept it. But they had not, and certainly would not, and that was the end of it. When I returned to my assistant lectureship, it was to console myself for a truly terrible performance.

It was six weeks later when I received a letter of appointment from the Zoo. I was being offered £800 a year, plus the occupancy of a small flat in the Zoological Gardens. Astonished, I considered this extraordinary sequel to the interview's 'flop', and then, almost immediately, decided to accept.

I and the tiger were to make each other's acquaintance, after all: but first I would have to learn to catch the beast!

3. Send It to the Sanny

I was appointed Curator of Mammals and Veterinary Officer to the London Zoo on 1st October, 1951. On the same day John Yealland was appointed Curator of Birds.

Despite the resonance of the titles we were, both of us, very much the new boys on the first day of term when we arrived – punctually, on the stroke of nine – at the office of the Zoo Superintendent, at that time the inimitable George Cansdale.

Furthermore, although we were received with the greatest kindness, it soon became plain that there were certain factors regarding my status and responsibilities that might make my job somewhat less portentous than it sounded.

When Cansdale took Yealland and me around the main offices to introduce us to other members of the staff, I sensed that he was somewhat at a loss as to how to define my own particular duties and 'spheres of influence,' and it was not long before I realised the reason for the Superintendent's apparent vagueness.

As I was the first veterinary surgeon ever to be employed by the Zoo in a full-time residential capacity, Cansdale had no precedent to guide him, and neither had I: we had to learn as we progressed the demarcations of the role, and the many and diverse demands that would be made upon it. But probably another factor to lend a touch of uncertainty to the business, was the unknown effect of my appointment on the existing veterinary staff.

At that time, the Zoo's hospital arrangements were confined exclusively to the outdated facilities afforded by the Old Sanatorium – universally known as the 'Sanny'. This was manned by a devoted but overworked and ill-equipped staff, who did their best with very poor tools, and had few of the advantages that stem from 'influence' or status. Just how, it may have been wondered, would we get on together?

It wasn't long before it appeared to me that 'send it to the Sanny' was the order that was given as the last resort – to dispose of sick animals that had failed to respond to a Head Keeper's ideas of treatment and looked like dying on him.

Hard though the idea may seem, this attitude was not solely activated by esteem for the sanatorium's record of cures, but it stemmed mainly from considerations of prestige and professional propriety. Each Head Keeper kept his books with meticulous care, and disliked a death among his charges as much as a surgeon hates to admit to D.O.T. – or Death on Table.

In the past, there were rumours prevalent that some surgeons, when convinced their best efforts had failed, were not above rushing their hopeless patients, duly sutured, back to the wards, in order to preserve their records from the embarrassment associated with D.O.T. It appeared that in some sections of the London Zoo a like philosophy might prevail as regards sick animals for whom hope had been abandoned. Small wonder that the instruction to 'send it to the Sanny' should assume at times the dreadful finality of a Death Sentence.

How was it possible for this practice to become established among people who would fight to the limit of their energies,

Send It to the Sanny

and experience, to maintain the health of the creatures under their care? Just why was the Sanatorium so demonstrably unsuccessful in its subsequent efforts at treatment?

To answer such questions it is necessary to describe the place as it was with 'warts and all.' But to maintain a balanced opinion of the 'Sanny's' defects, it should not be forgotten that the facilities it provided – limited though they were – were still more comprehensive than those offered anywhere else in the world.

The old sanatorium lay low along the southernmost tip of the Zoo's most easterly border. As such, it could be said to have been nicely positioned with a view that would have extended across one of the most pleasant aspects of Regent's Park – were it not for the detail that its two-storey buildings looked inwards! Surveying only of its own kind overlooking the large collecting yard where animals arrived in boxes and crates for transfer, the Sanny's outlook was indeed restricted. The yard's boundaries to the south were flanked by the Prosectorium, and the offices and laboratories of the Prosector. Next to its entrance and exit was the First Aid and Nursing Mother's Room, and, in strange juxtaposition, one of the buildings labelled 'Gentlemen.'

The 'Sanny' was probably among the oldest of the Zoo's very old buildings, and appeared to have been created out of a row of haylofts, cart sheds and stables, the latter of which surely must have housed the originally horsed transport of the Zoo, and probably dated back for nearly a century.

There was an air of almost desperate improvisation about the place, and much laudable effort had been expended to make the most of very little. The long-ranging haylofts had been converted into accommodation for 'small animals' in cages, and what had once formed the grooms' cramped quarters had been turned into an office together with another small room which acted as clinic cum dressing room, cum operating theatre, cum anything you like!

Access to these floors was severely limited, and consisted of the traditional mews-style steps, while the ground floor was given over to 'large animals' who – lions included! – were housed in ex-horse boxes, or in dens which, in many cases, still had stable doors. Some of these had been reinforced because of the security risk, others had steel bars on the doors, and all of them were isolated, one from the other. There was little or no provision for a keeper's entry – or escape! – by covered way from cell to cell. Nor was there any form of exercise paddock. In the main, the animals could only be approached by way of the front door, which meant that, for the purpose of effective examination, let alone treatment, they could hardly be approached at all!

Such, then, was the 'Sanny' less than twenty years ago . . . the animal medical centre of the world's greatest zoo . . . the unpublicised part of a scientific institution and all-star attraction to visitors from every country in the globe. But what of the problems of those who worked in its ancient buildings; the small group who did their best in impossible conditions?

When I first visited the 'Sanny' it was not only completely lacking in suitable accommodation and scientific equipment – it was overcrowded, and very much understaffed.

There were over sixty animals in the 'Sanny' itself, and another twenty sick were in the Gardens: some of them were very ill indeed.

To administer to the medical needs of this hapless collection of patients, and keep their accommodation as clean as was humanly possible, was the job of a staff that totalled only five: one of whom was the Sanatorium Super-

Send It to the Sanny

visor. Needless to say, the morale of these much-strained men was very low.

How, I wondered, had this unfortunate situation come about? I was answered by an explanation that, somewhat bitterly, was inclined to lay blame on the doorstep of some of the Head Keepers. At that time these men exerted a hierarchial sway, and the decisions they made on the animals in their care was regarded as almost infallible. A Head Keeper, so it seemed, could do no wrong.

The house was *his*, its occupants were *his*, and to keep them in splendid health was *his* privilege and pride. The glossier the coat, the clearer the eye – the brighter was his personal image reflected, proudly shining. The rule of the Head Keepers, established by the usage of decades, was a highly personalised affair, with overtones of the patriarchs, and the caste system too.

It would be impossible to deny that the regime of these highly experienced men was in many respects quite excellent. The young keepers, their acolytes, shared in their glory, which, based as it was on hard work and efficiency, was no bad thing to emulate. Elan was high, and loyalties were fierce. Yet it was in the very source of its strength – its insistence that the criteria of excellence were in the health and fine grooming of the individual animal – that the system held the seed of a weakness.

In the absence of an authoritative medical service, initially it was the Head Keeper on whom fell the task of deciding what was wrong with an animal and what steps to take concerning its treatment. Based largely on the grounds that he probably knew more about the animal and its behaviour than anyone else – this prescription was often justified by results. But, there were occasions when the process went seriously wrong.

First Catch Your Tiger

There was, for example, the type of Head Keeper who would contribute to the 'Sanny's' overcrowding by sending it his charges prematurely, rather than 'scandalise the neighbours' by the presence of a sick animal in his house. And there was also – the complete opposite – the Head Keeper who would endeavour to obscure the animal's condition until the last moment, when, its position desperate, he would send it to the sanatorium lest it die while 'on his books' and in his care. At such times the 'Sanny' became a dumping ground for the unwanted, the difficult or the tedious.

'Send it to the "Sanny" . . .' With the best will in the world it was impossible for the place to cope with the demands that were made upon it, given the staff and the facilities available. Nobody so far had made a thorough study of the clinical conditions of captive wild animals, and how those conditions arose – far less had therapy been tackled. There was no record of precedent to turn to regarding treatment and cure. For the 'Sanny's' staff there was seldom a word of thanks.

Practically nothing was known about the difficulties under which they worked, or the efforts that they made to overcome them. Their prestige was nil.

A young keeper in the Lion House could proudly boast 'I am a lion man!' – and this would really mean something among his keen contemporaries. The appointment smacked of drama, and gave birth to prideful colloquialisms, 'I'm with the Big Cats' and all the rest of it – but what was there to romanticise over the staff in the 'Sanny?' The Zoo's staff structures literally reeked of caste distinction, or, perhaps more accurately, a regimental spirit which, while all very splendid for the men of the 'crack' formations, was rather rough on the others!

Send It to the Sanny

The men of the 'Sanny' certainly had little to commend their lot. They lacked even the not inconsiderable benefits of the tipping system, which produced a welcome addition to the salaries of other members of the uniformed staff. Such tips came from the visiting public – and of course no member of the public could be admitted to the 'Sanny'!

Shortly after my arrival – and provoked by the definitive comment from one quarter that 'we don't talk about *sick* animals in the Zoo' – I interviewed, at some length, the Sanatorium staff, and found them excellent quality, even though so obviously disheartened. They confessed to me that the job was so unpopular that nobody volunteered for it, and that replacements and reinforcements had to be 'posted,' for the 'Sanny', I gradually appreciated, was considered as tantamount to the military Glass House. It bore the stigma of being a place where nobody who was any good would want to go.

Probably the main thing wrong with the place reflected an inherited impression, dating back in all probability to the Zoo's foundation that to admit to the presence of sick animals was to confess to something shameful. It was as if only negligence could be responsible for one of its 6,000 strong population falling ill!

This astonishing misconception needed immediate correction, and I decided to start off by establishing the principle that a certain amount of illness among the Zoo's huge collection of animals was as inevitable as the fact that night follows day and could be defeated by the same processes that we apply to illness in man, among them the prompt notification of occurrence, so that diagnosis can be attempted at an early stage.

Not everyone, however, found this to be glaringly

First Catch Your Tiger

obvious, and the process of conversion was to take longer than I thought.

At a time when I was almost friendless, and was rightly suspected all round as having not the slightest practical experience of wild animals and their behaviour, I was fortunate in acquiring the whole-hearted support of the men in the 'Sanny', even though they may have regarded my plans as super-optimistic: an exercise of hope against experience!

Together, I decided, we would establish a veterinary service that would embrace the whole Zoo in its activities. We would set up a system whereby any variation in an animal's health would be reported to us as soon as it occurred; and where the diagnosis and treatment of an illness would be the responsibility of the service, and of the service alone. We would, of course, honour and indeed welcome the views of the Head Keepers, who, with their practical experience of the individual animal and its reactions to circumstances, could render invaluable service. But there must be an end to piecemeal doctoring by unqualified practitioners, whose efforts were often haphazard and largely unrecorded.

As a first move in what may now seem to be no more than an exercise in common sense, but was regarded as an absolutely revolutionary innovation, I decided to establish a daily (early morning) tour of the Gardens from the 'Sanny'.

In the course of this the Sanatorium Supervisor was able to make his own observations on the condition of the animals in general, and receive verbal information from the keeper staff. Also the Head Keepers would report their health returns by telephone – all reports being completed by 9.00 a.m. the Sanatorium Supervisor, having returned from his inspection, could confer with me on the appropriate action.

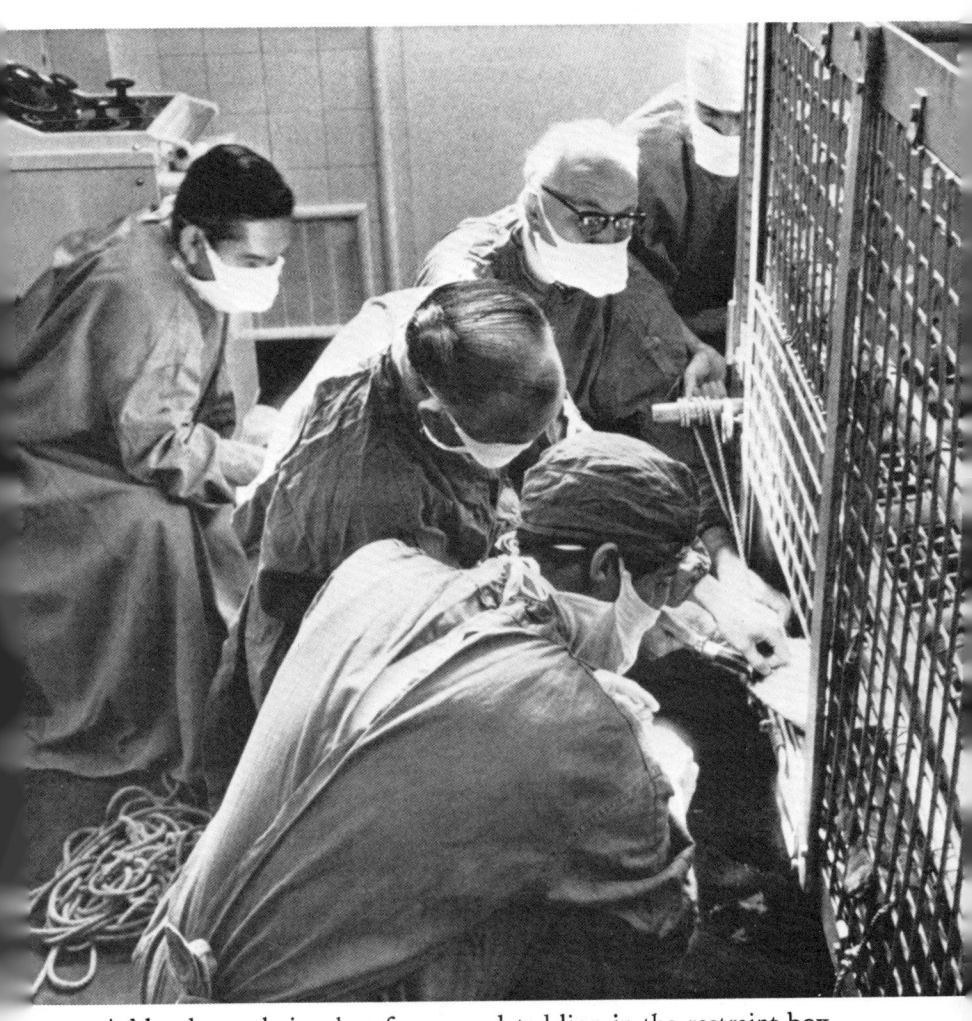

A blood sample is taken from a sedated lion in the restraint box.

The toucan's severed lower bill.

The artificial lower bill showing the metal cutting edge.

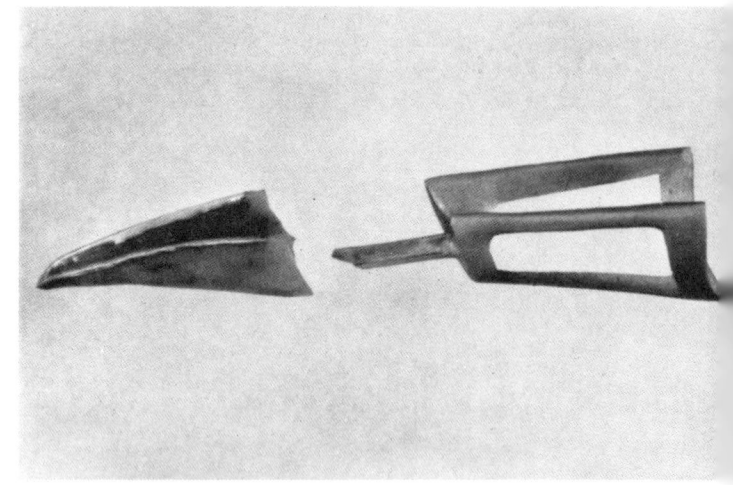

The bill fitted.

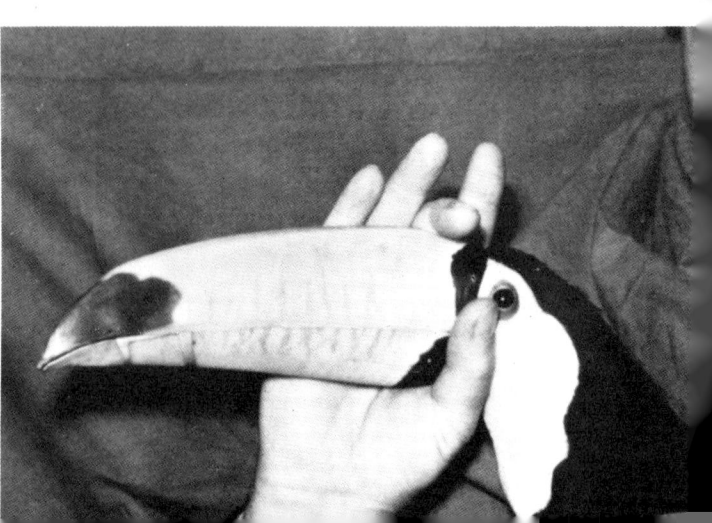

A very sedated bear which has rolled into the undergrowth. The arrow indicates the anaesthetic dart.

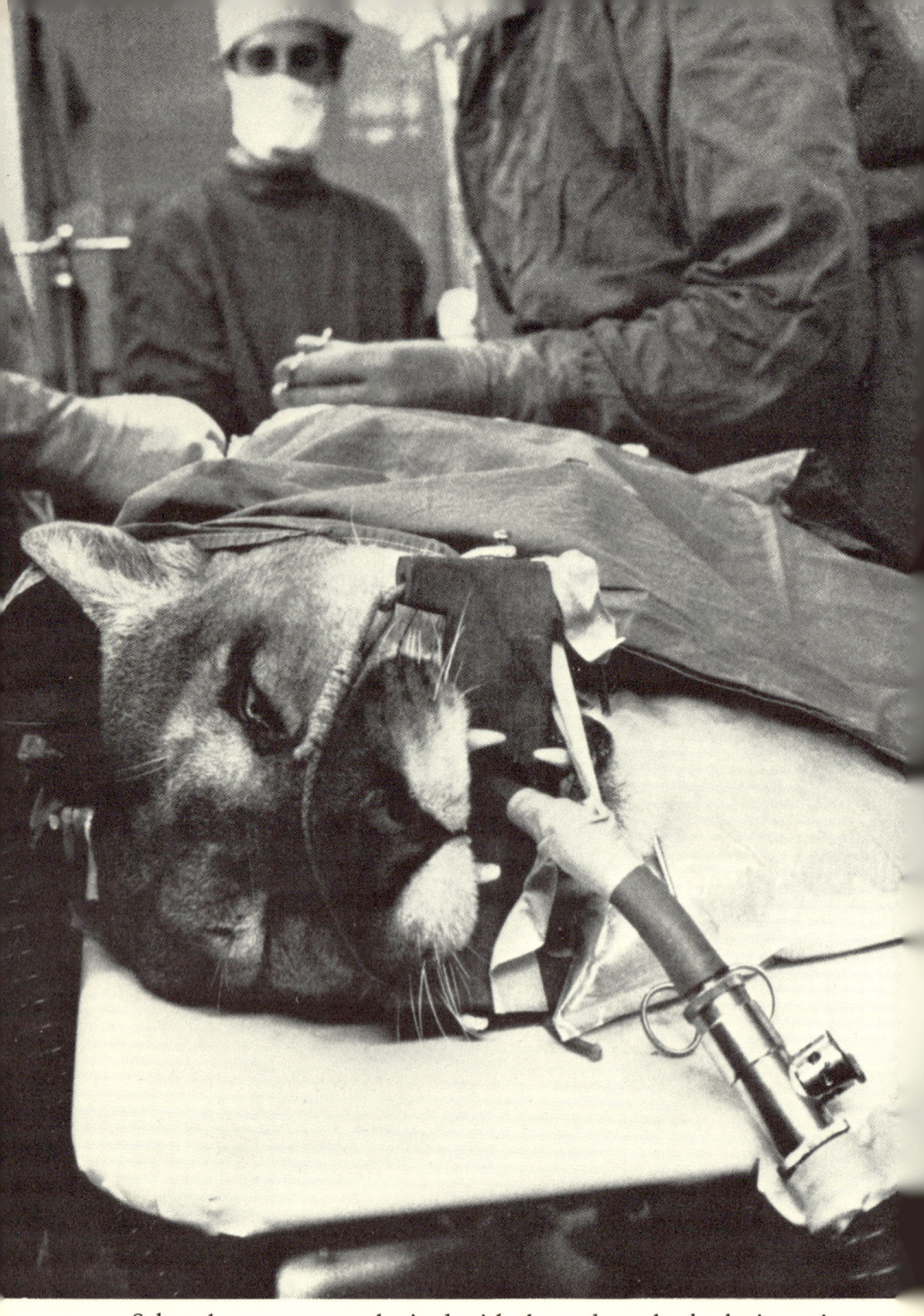

Sabre the puma anaesthetised with the endotracheal tube in position.

Send It to the Sanny

Looking back, the necessity for some such form of disciplined routine seems so elementary that it is difficult to recall the intensity of feeling that it aroused in certain quarters. Yet, it was perhaps understandable that there should have been some resentment – not entirely confined to the keepers – of the fact that the new Veterinary Officer was asserting his appointment. Some even regarded it as empire building!

To the plaints of this not uninfluential opposition, I resolved, however, to turn an extremely deaf ear, and was ably supported in this respect by the Sanatorium Supervisor who, despite the fact that his tour involved him in bearing the brunt each day of the lower echelons' blunt criticisms, remained both cool and loyal, and immensely tactful with it, too!

We took the view that, given time and success, we would win the goodwill of even the most obdurate of the keepers, and that once our service could show its worth, it would not only become acceptable, but welcome. And in this respect our optimism was to prove fully justified.

Today, the London Zoo leads the world in many ways including the efficiency of its sickness early-warning system. An example of the benefits that can arise from close teamwork between keepers and hospital staff, this ensures that an illness can be treated at its earliest stage, before it has managed to secure a grip upon the patient, and thus is the more susceptible to treatment. In fact the system of preventive medicine that has been developed assists in negating illness before it starts.

*

The early notification of disease . . . the establishment of good hygiene . . . a series of fairly simple – but morale-building surgical operations . . . such were the early stepping-stones towards drastically renovating the Zoo's medical service, and altering the general attitude towards it. Next came our lobbying for equipment, for at that time we had next to nothing.

Proper portable cages, to transport wild animals from their house to the hospital, and from their hospital dens to the operating theatre, were almost unheard of. Radiography facilities – essential for any detailed examination of a patient – were nil. There was no X-ray machine. Medical records – with the invaluable precedents they provide – were grotesquely incomplete. We pressed as hard as we could to be provided with them, and where we could not we turned to improvisation.

But while these individual problems could be fought over, and eventually overcome – although sometimes by processes that were laborious and seemed time-wasting – there was one major obstacle that could only be removed by means of a massive injection of cash, and cash – in the Zoo of the time – was a commodity that seemed to be in short supply.

The problem? The 'Sanny' itself. We decided it must be rebuilt, and not only rebuilt but moved; and this not solely because of the need for accommodating the animals in dens where it would be possible to examine them in depth, but also for the sake of security, and the need to prevent the spread of epidemic disease. It was essential to provide a new hospital completely and, having done so, to devise methods of using it to its utmost.

As it was, the old sanatorium could not have been worse sited in respect of the security and infection risks it posed to the Zoo at large. Even the wildest specimens had to be brought to it from the transport point in the outer circle,

Send It to the Sanny

and any diseased animals had to be passed through the zoo at its thickest – and most populated – part. The danger of escape, or epidemic, was therefore a very real one, and was constantly a source of apprehension to us.

Yet another grave risk was posed by the great quantities of dung deposited by the animals from the Gardens. The problems of disposing of this possible source of disease were being aggravated by what used to be called The March of Science!

For many years it had been the custom for the major part of the Zoo's animal waste to be taken away by contractors for disposal on the soil, but then had come the post-war boom in artificial fertilisers and, with a lessening demand for the natural product, we could see that eventually we would be faced with a situation that would not only be embarrassing, but might also present a very real danger to health. Also we had to consider the point that, in a foot and mouth disease scare, bans on transport could make collection and disposal difficult, if not impossible. The dung pound build-up could become alarming.

'Science' had also created difficulties over another unpleasant and not-much-talked-about problem, the disposal of dead animals. Animal fat, hitherto used for a multitude of unlikely purposes – including, so it was whispered, a type of beauty-aid – now had a synthetic counterpart, so in this sphere too, 'demand' was falling off. This left us with the alternative of cremation, but then, to complicate matters further, there came the need to conform to the requirements of the new smokeless zone. Conceivably this could have been done by our increasing the chimney heights above our furnace, but this in turn was ruled out by the Town and Country Planning Acts!

Such problems as these, unsavoury though they were,

First Catch Your Tiger

were not such as could be ignored, or even shelved. In the interests of hygiene, and of amenities in general, someone had to find a solution, and find it fairly fast, and in the end the task in small part devolved on us.

This meant that, in addition to fulfilling the tasks normally associated with the veterinary profession, I found myself in the somewhat ghoulish – and certainly unsought – role of visitor to one of the most modern of London's crematoria.

There, together with the architects, I learned the most efficient methods of disposal, and studied the use of afterburners, which effectively destroyed the original smoke.

Interesting though this process may have been, it was with considerable relief that I was able to turn from the study of disposal of the dead, and resume planning what we would need in the way of facilities to help the living.

When I had made my first contact with the 'Sanny', it did not possess an ambulance. Sick animals had to be conveyed to it in the trucks of the transport section, or upon very noisy flat steel low loaders. There were no detailed records of the animal's health background, no case history at all. Isolation facilities were minimal, and neither was there any really comprehensive system of security that I could detect in the Gardens at all. 'Advanced' though the very idea of a sanatorium might have been, in the sense that few zoos in the world could offer even the rudimentary treatment given by London, its service was at Florence Nightingale level when compared with the scientific resources and techniques that had become involved in human medicine and nursing.

But now what had seemed at times to be a pipe-dream – the demise of the old 'Sanny' and its replacement by a hospital that would be on a scale commensurate with the zoo's tremendous prestige – was fast becoming fact.

To their everlasting credit, the Zoo authorities had

recognised the 'Sanny's' shortcomings, and had made an appropriation of funds to plan and build a modern zoo animal hospital: the best-equipped zoo animal hospital in the world.

The lease of the old Quarantine Station at Gloucester Gate was due to fall through, and it had been decided to launch a development scheme that would combine Quarantine facilities, Hospital and Laboratories, all in one compactly grouped establishment.

We were moving on, and in more senses than one.

4. Animal Hospital

'You have too much of the Celt in you, and you must learn to control it!'

Before detailing the facilities the new hospital had to offer, and the types of problems we found inherent in the treatment of wild animals, it is necessary to depart from the strictly chronological in order to convey some idea of the circumstances in which our plans had germinated.

Opposition to our interpretation of the responsibilities of the health service had by no means been confined exclusively to the keepers, and the end of my year's probation had brought me a word of warning from Viscount Chaplin, at that time the Secretary, and a man for whom I had the greatest liking and respect.

Coming from such a source, the remark had stung me, and I demanded to know if there had been any complaints about the way in which I had tackled the job itself. If there were – and the charges were justified – I was prepared to resign.

It transpired, however, that I had been accused of 'getting people's backs up', and involved in 'rows' and that Lord Chaplin's words had been meant as a gentle warning that I could make life easier for myself and others by being a little more diplomatic in my handling of 'local interests.'

He was ready, however, to recommend confirmation of my appointment subject to another 12 months' probation

Animal Hospital

and our association was to be on a pleasant and understanding basis until the day of his retirement. Some people in honesty wondered if I was temperamentally suited to the appointment.

In the early days of experiment and trial not all of my relationships at the Zoo were on such a friendly footing.

From the very start – when both the President of the R.C.V.S. and the Dean of the R.V.C. took the trouble separately to interview me – it was abundantly clear that the appointment was regarded as a new venture for the profession in general, and my success or failure would be of more than purely personal interest. But even then I had not realised that I was to play in effect the role of catalyst in a process that was likely to be resented.

The decision of the Zoo authorities to employ a resident veterinary surgeon had been made perhaps by some with doubts, and perhaps was influenced by the legislation contained in the 1948 Veterinary Surgeons Acts, which basically made it an offence for anyone other than a veterinary surgeon to diagnose and treat disease in animals.

It seems curious that the provisions of the Act did not – and still do not – apply to the actual owner of animals. Thus it is possible that the Zoo, as 'owner' of the animals in its care, could have continued to operate very much as it had before, and that it did not, is very much to its credit.

All the same there could well have been some heart-burning at what was rightly regarded as the end of a tradition as old as the place itself; a tradition moreover that had resulted in the growth of various vested interests. It was not long before I had a taste of the influence these exerted.

As the first member of my profession to enter a sphere

First Catch Your Tiger

habitually reserved for the zoologist, I was naturally the subject of a good deal of attention, and speculation too. On the part of some members of the Zoo's establishment, curiosity was blended with goodwill, not to mention a wry sympathy! – to others the introduction of a 'Vet' smacked of gross interference. In their view a real bounder had been admitted to the club!

With the unique facilities it provided for scientific study and research – facilities unknown to comparable establishments abroad – the London Zoo had attracted over the years and continues to attract some of the most eminent personalities in the field of science, zoology, and conservation. Yet, to meet the medical requirements of its huge animal population, it had been content in the past to rely on the ad hoc employment of veterinary officers with outside practices, and had called on them rather as a householder calls on the fire brigade – namely when the blaze has actually gained a hold. Previously two attempts had been made to employ a veterinary surgeon on a non-resident basis but there were very great difficulties.

With no resident adviser, and no centralised direction in organising a health regime, practically the only time when 'advanced' techniques of surgery were employed was when those skilled in the practice of human medicine indulged a desire to dabble in the veterinary field.

In fact to certain of the eminent names who had established themselves in the councils of the Zoo, the 'Vet' was a hick from the sticks, with bog myrtle coming out of his ears. To some, he remains just that!

On the other hand I was in a perpetual state of surprise – and did not hesitate to show it – at the undeniable fact that, so very little in terms of money and effort was being directed to the general improvement of the health of the animals whose behaviour had attracted so much interest from those intent on zoological study and research.

To me it seemed quite extraordinary that we would spend a minor furtune in purchasing a captive wild animal and bringing it half-way across the world, and yet not provide more than the most basic facilities for its medical care on arrival, and the maintenance of its health thereafter.

My views in this respect were echoed by the hospital staff, and the keepers gladly gave us their cooperation once they found that our ideas 'worked'. However, there were others on a higher plane who were more difficult to handle.

Despite the efforts of those who were anxious to ensure a harmonious working relationship between all branches of the Zoo's activities, we, whose primary responsibility was for the health of the animals, were moving on a collision course with some of the hierarchy, and the time came when we duly collided.

The crunch came with the publication of a feature that was to become part of one of the Zoo's committee's established routines, but was considered on its advent to be almost revolutionary.

When animals died it was the responsibility of the Prosectorial Committee to decide on the allocation of their bodies. Whether they went to the researchers – both national and international – or were consigned to the museum, or the disposal merchants, was the affair of the committee and the committee alone. The numbers of the dead, and the species to which they belonged, was published in the committee's periodic report, but this gave no details of the reasons contributing to death, and neither was there any assessment of measures that could possibly have prevented the animal's demise. I felt that this was just not good enough, and decided that the omission ought to be rectified.

My request granted, I prepared the first of a series of quarterly reports that gave not only the number and species of animals who had been treated by the veterinary service, but also contained the numbers of those who had been admitted to the 'Sanny', together with information as to the nature of their illnesses, their treatment, and their ultimate fate. It also carried my personal comments on the need for cooperation between the veterinary service and other branches of the Zoo, particularly stressing, in this instance, the Prosectorium.

I had been amazed to learn of the relatively high percentage of the population which crossed the post mortem table annually, particularly the newly arrived – and I wanted to know why!

A little later I attended a meeting of the Prosectorial Committee at which a very distinguished professor was Chairman. Frostily he glanced at my observations, turned over the pages, and then slammed them on to the table with the words 'I decline to read this report!'

There was an awkward silence broken by a gentle statement to the effect that the report carried council's authority, but the Chairman merely answered, with finality, 'There is no obligation for me to accept or circulate this report, and I shall not do so.'

Neither did he.

This attitude seemed suddenly to crystallise the opinions of some colleagues who regarded the veterinary profession's intervention as less than an advantage and much of a nuisance. It was also an extreme manifestation of the suspicion felt by more moderate opponents of our health

Animal Hospital

service – namely that our function might impinge their work in other fields. However, the occasion demanded, or so I felt, something more in consideration of the other fellow's point of view. Defeat on one point could mean defeat on all.

With this in mind I pursued the issue to a cleavage, and brought my complaints to the highest level, and eventually, after a skirmish whose details would be fruitless to recall, the affair served to clear the air and led to a better understanding all round. When, at the next meeting of the Prosectorial Committee, I presented the second of my quarterly reports, it received a very different reception from its predecessor. It was read out to the members and – more importantly – so also was the offending 'first'.

A battle had been won, but the pity of it was that it had had to be fought at all.

After meeting so much opposition during the first two years' existence of the veterinary service, the decision to go ahead in building the Zoo hospital marked for those of us who had laboured in the vineyard far more than the realisation of a hope that had been nurtured by necessity, namely the inadequacy of the 'Sanny.' It also represented – or so I like to think – the beginning of a comprehensive system of collaboration between ourselves and all possible branches of those sciences concerned with the study of captive wild animals.

At the time of the hospital's conception we knew that misgivings were circulating regarding its cost and nature. We knew also that there were doubts about the need for certain of the amenities we planned to offer the animals: our 'pretensions,' too, had come under heavy criticism. The Zoo authorities had long been aware of the need for the new hospital, but I think that in the long run it was only the realisation that they could combine this with the new quarantine post and the pathological laboratories – grouping these departments all under one roof so to speak – that freed the funds that were necessary for a project as comprehensive as the one we planned.

For various reasons, the negotiations leading up to the authorities' decisions were confidential – and possibly still are – and the hospital, even as it exists today, is somewhat short of what we had originally hoped for. This said, however, there is no doubt that the Zoological Society has provided an institution that is worthy of its status, and will be adequate for the health needs of its animals far into the foreseeable future.

Designed by the Zoological Society's architect, the hospital can compare favourably with any contemporary institution for the medical care of humans. It can cater for approximately 98 per cent of the Zoo's inmates – mammalian, avian and reptilian – and has facilities for the most complex operations and the most advanced methods of treatment.

The roomy dens that line the corridors of the first floor can offer not only isolation, but comfort, to twenty-one of the big animals, and there is recreation and exercise space as well.

Giraffes, elephants, and hippos obviously are among the very few patients who have to face their problems in their own surroundings, but even to these the hospital is important: their treatment being much improved by the experience acquired within its walls.

When we first started to dream our dreams of a replacement for the 'Sanny', there was not even proper transport

Animal Hospital

available to move the animals from their cages. Today they travel to the hospital in an electrically powered ambulance, specially equipped for their comfort and security: and this is just one instance among many of the way in which things have altered for the better.

In hospitals designed for the care of man great emphasis is laid on the need to maintain the patient's confidence – the Napoleonic axiom of morale's superiority to the material being never more apt than when applied to the battle against disease.

But high morale in an animal has usually to be induced by recourse to the material, in which is included the provision of an environment that it finds agreeable. A sick animal can lose the 'will to live' far more readily than man, with his capacity to understand the reassurances of his doctors, and his introspection lightened by amenities – books, television and so forth – to ease his boredom and sedate his fears.

To remedy this deficiency of the animal we employed frequent changes of diet, offering them dishes that normally they would get only as delicacies. A fresh air balcony was provided, to give sick patients a view of the world outside during the period of their rehabilitation. And last, but by no means least, we encouraged frequent visiting. The sight of someone who is familiar to it – and that normally means its keeper – often does more for a sick animal's morale than any amount of medicine. Very seldom did we find a keeper who was reluctant to visit his charge!

Despite the controversy surrounding its inception the benefits bestowed by the hospital and its vital accessory the Veterinary Service are today accepted, and well appreciated. But it is perhaps inevitable that the innovation that has brought it the most prestige is its highly modern,

First Catch Your Tiger

fully equipped operating theatre. The generic struggles are – perhaps rightly – forgotten by all.

The first recorded operation ever to be conducted at the Zoo was on a baboon with a decaying tooth, and took place in 1837, within nine years of the Zoo's opening. Interestingly indicative of the forward-looking attitude of the visiting veterinary surgeon was the fact that the extraction was performed under an anaesthetic. The Zoo's first operation on a large animal, carried out just a little later, was more in keeping with the spirit of its time.

To extract an ulcerated tusk from a giant hippo three men hauled on a pair of forceps two feet long – across a fence erected to protect them from their patient!

In the present day we do things rather differently, but there is always a very real risk – both to the patient and surgeon – that is absent from operations conducted on man.

A domestic animal has accustomed itself to man and his environment, and will submit to being modestly disciplined or restrained. A wild animal is governed only by the means of self-preservation – flight, defence and attack – and its reaction to even the slightest attempt at discipline will be savage, and mercilessly swift. Additionally it will have sustained considerable shock, and this in turn will induce clinical reactions of disturbance and distress. Thus the pre-requisite of any attempt at treatment must be a method of restraint that will be immediately or speedily effective, and yet, at the same time, will subject the animal to the minimum degree of dangerous stress.

Even when anaesthetics are employed this has not always been an easy objective, as witness the following alarming description by Severinghaus, written as recently as 1950.

Describing the manual restraint of a deer, emerging from

a catching crate, he writes: 'The catcher had to tackle it in such a manner that his right hand passed under its neck to stop the forward motion, while his left went over its back to hold it down. Simultaneously he threw his weight against the deer's shoulder hard enough to knock it off balance. As the animal fell, the catcher threw his body and legs across its back so as to avoid the threshing hooves, and then slid his left hand along its neck.' At a later stage of this complicated exercise which the author describes in such detail that it verges on the incomprehensible, 'the catcher's body was sprawled horizontally along the deer's back, and his legs were free. His right leg was then placed across the animal's flank and he hooked his foot in front of one of the deer's hind feet.'

The immediate prelude to anaesthesia was when an assistant approached the deer from the rear, and 'pressing his chest over its hip,' worked his hands down its hind legs until he had grasped both of the animal's hind feet. 'The deer was held in this position by two men while the anaesthetic was injected into the saphenous vein by a third person.'

Well, so much for anaesthesia as it used to be! And so the dictum that an animal, while being subjected to anaesthesia, must be protected from the influence of excitement and stress!

Our own methods of restraining a patient in order to bring it to the operating table were definitely less demanding on the muscles, although probably far less dramatic as regards the degree of acrobatic skill employed. Clearly I was a coward!

*

The role of Veterinary Officer was exacting enough in

First Catch Your Tiger

itself, but to combine it with that of the Curator of Mammals was an arduous complication. As Curator I found myself confronted by matters involving aspects of administration that contrasted oddly with my purely veterinary work. Promotions and transfers . . . the acquisition of new staff . . . these were just part of the responsibilities of the job. Waste disposal and the provision of fodder supply also came under my jurisdiction. Add to this tally the fact that matters affecting the exhibition and display of all mammals also concerned me, and it will be appreciated that at times the job induced a hint of schizophrenia.

It was, therefore, to my intense relief that eventually the two posts separated: with Desmond Morris (of *Naked Ape* fame) taking over as Curator, and myself being left free to concentrate on the challenge presented by the needs of my panel; over six thousand wild animals controlled by nearly three hundred keepers.

Looking back on that period – a period in which eagerness and trepidation were almost equally balanced, and sometimes interwoven – I do not think that I can exaggerate the extent of my ignorance of the requirements of these patients, or the problems involved in their diagnosis and treatment; problems literally poles apart from those associated with the domestic pet. I had, of course, done my best to inform myself, but literature on the subject was almost non-existent. I had been able to obtain only the most superficial information on the general habits of the animals and their characteristics when exposed to sickness or distress, and the complications of adjusting surgical techniques developed primarily for man, to creatures of the wild, had not really been appreciated by me until I came face to face with those I had to treat.

5. Patients Extraordinary

Sedating a three ton hippo that had quarrelled with its mate . . . replacing a male toucan's beak, bitten off by a female of the species . . . coping with a T.B. outbreak among the tenants of Monkey Hill . . . had we been able to foresee in those early days of innocence and ignorance, the sort of problems that were to confront us in the decade ahead, we might perhaps have been less sure in our confidence that the veterinary service could successfully tackle the myriad health needs of the Zoo's inhabitants. Equally with precious hindsight we might have been less vocally indignant at the shortcomings of the old order, but, as it was, we had to learn the hard way; and the first thing we learned was the width of the gulf between the things you could do in human therapy and the things it was practical to do with a wild animal, where reactions were in complete contrast to those of man.

It is all very well to plan an operation on a tiger, but the problem that arises is how to catch the beast, and, once having caught it, how safely to secure it. Nor is this difficulty restricted to the tiger, it applies in lesser or greater degree to every type of wild animal in captivity. Not one of them will cooperate in your well-meaning efforts to help them, and no such thing as gratitude exists in their primitive make-up.

When treating a human, the doctor is able to enlist his patient as an ally. His diagnosis is based not only on his

First Catch Your Tiger

observations of the latter's condition, but also on what the patient is able to tell him. How he feels . . . the type of discomfort he suffers from . . . normally the sick man is only too willing to talk about his symptoms.

With a domestic animal, accustomed to man – and looking to him to meet his every need – diagnosis is also relatively easy. It is possible to examine the patient at close range, and conduct tests, take temperatures, auscultate, palpate, peer into mouth and eyes and feel the pulse. It is possible to ask the owner questions about the animal's appetite, functions, its general behaviour and so forth. These diagnostic aids are available and invaluable too.

But what do you do – and where do you start – when your patient is pure savage, a terrified powerful creature of the wild? When, far from welcoming your ministrations it reacts with violence to them, and has the capacity to kill?

The wild animal, when sick, is inevitably a 'loner,' moreover it is a loner that sometimes has homicidal instincts. Its disability hampers the mobility of the herd, and it has all the guilt of one that's now unwanted by its fellows. In such circumstances it will express its fears and depression in agonised, and agonising, hatred when confronted by the human intruder; venting its fury on him, tooth and claw.

So how do you get such a patient to the operating table? Not all the charm in Harley Street can induce it to come by persuasion. You have to bring it against its will or bring it not at all. And what precautions do you adopt on the way – remembering that your purpose is to cure the angry animal, not to kill it by the very efforts directed to helping it? Just how do you anaesthetise him when you get him there, and prepare him for a surgical operation? You can't tell a tiger to relax and breathe in gently while you adjust the drapes and – so to speak – turn on the tap!

When confronted by questions such as these, I found that, elementary though they might well appear to be, nobody had felt fit to provide a detailed answer to them. Nor could we glean more than the most rudimentary fragments of information as to the way in which current trends in human medicine and care could be related to our animals. We had indeed to learn the hard way.

But the factor of restraint – the problem of securing your animal so that it can be subjected to surgery without doing harm to you – or itself – in the process, is only one part of the problem. Undoubtedly it is a very big part of the problem, but it is still not the whole of it; the need for sedation and anaesthesia runs it a very close second. What proportion of a man orientated dose of sedatives do you offer, say, an injured budgerigar? How many gallons of medicament are considered to be adequate for an elephant? Alas, search though I did through the textbooks, I could find almost nothing that could act as a precedent for us to follow. It just hadn't been comprehensively recorded, even if done.

Neither was there an abundance of comprehensive information on the behavioural patterns of wild animals in captivity. I discovered that under the stress of sickness, or its treatment, animals differed very widely one from another in their reactions, and were even less predictable than man in what they required to build up their morale.

Lorenz, Hediger, Morris and others have done much to explain many of the mechanisms of the inter- and intra-specific relationships of many animals, much of which gave us a good understanding of the basis of many of our problems of emerging disease in captive wild animals.

First Catch Your Tiger

Surprises of physiology ... surprises of psychology ... they were to be sprung on us in plenty as we sought to establish norms for diagnosis and treatment; and sometimes our ignorance had tragic results.

One of the earliest of all our operations in the 'Sanny' was performed on a small fat honey-bear who had injured his paw; the wound later turning septic.

At that time, the Zoo's only method of getting an animal to the operating table was to carry it there, enmeshed in a capture-net, a factor that served only to increase its fear and stress.

The equipment for anaesthesia was equally primitive. To cater for the population of the world's largest collection of captive animals we had only one old leather face-mask, of the type once employed on race-horses, and a single bottle of chloroform. Anaesthesia was administered by the simple device of impregnating with the chloroform a thick wad of cotton wool, which was then slipped into a slide at the far end of the mask; subsequently clapped over the animal's head.

All in all, it was a most unreliable arrangement, and one that made me thankful for the fact that the surgical issues involved in the operation itself were of the simplest, and therefore our patient's lot should be far from critical. Unfortunately, however, we were to be faced by a factor of which I knew next to nothing – a physiological factor that was to have the most unexpected consequences.

In all respects, other than its ending, the operation followed along the lines we had expected. The animal was anaesthetised, with apparent success, although I was somewhat puzzled at the length of time that passed before it became unconscious: for such a little bear, he seemed to take a lot of anaesthetising. Attending to the septic wound, and finding it free of complications, I cleansed it, and sutured it, and waited for the patient to come round.

Slowly he returned to consciousness, breathing quite normally, and then – to our astonishment – he died!

It later transpired that lacking a satisfactory method of control the chloroform had been absorbed into the animal's body fat, and stored there rather as ink is absorbed by blotting paper. Eventually, saturation point had been reached, and this dangerous content waited to be unloaded.

Thus when the animal had come round, and had emptied its lungs and bloodstream of the chloroform in the usual manner, its reaction seemed to offer no grounds for alarm. But the stress had created a physiological condition which caused the whole accumulation suddenly to be released. The chloroform had then emptied back into the unfortunate animal's bloodstream in too high a concentration.

Mercifully, such a happening would be extremely rare today, when an animal can be medicated before anaesthesia, and any peculiarity of its respiratory system can be identified in advance. We have moved far beyond the chloroform state, and are equipped with such refinements as monitoring systems, which give constant information about the patient's pulse rate, and the plasma CO_2 levels, and help regulate the quantities and flow of the gas into and out of the patient.

At the time of which I write, although it was so comparatively recent, such developments would have seemed as remote as the Mountains of the Moon.

*

Depressing failures, morale-raising successes, at first they were more or less equally matched in the dramas that were

First Catch Your Tiger

played out on the rough wooden structure that passed for an operating table in the 'theatre' we had created in the 'Sanny'. It was to be a long while yet before the tide was to swing in our favour.

Yet, however inadequate the facilities that the old place had to offer, it was mandatory that we should make the utmost use of them.

The needs of the animals could not be shelved while we waited for years for the promised hospital. Neither would the staff's morale have benefited from the adoption of a purely passive pose, in which we attempted only the simplest acts of surgery.

Like it or not – and we didn't! – the position was that, if we wanted to bring about any sort of significant improvement in the lot of the Zoo's sick, we must be prepared to take calculated risks, both with them and our reputations.

Thus, at an early stage, I decided to embark on a quite complex surgical exercise, by conducting an operation on an African civet cat.

In this case a Caesarean section had become necessary because of a transverse presentation of the emerging baby: its head instead of emerging from the mother's vagina had by-passed the proximal end of the cervix, and had traversed up the other uterine horn.

However, despite these complications, the operation was highly successful, and as one very live, and very healthy, kitten was eventually extracted from the patient, the story can be said to have had a satisfactorily happy ending. We did not, however, leave the pair to share the joys of the mother-daughter relationship. *That* was something that we did not dare to do.

The trouble was that the civet cat just couldn't be trusted.

Patients Extraordinary

She had been pregnant on previous occasions, and each time her kittens had mysteriously 'vanished.' She was, we now realised, a cannibal, and as such could not be left alone with her offspring. So we left the task of rearing our new arrival to a cocker spaniel bitch, who brought her up like one of her own.

Those early days were days in which we not only defined and listed our problems but accepted the fact that we must tackle them very largely on our own.

It soon became apparent that there was little sense in removing an animal from familiar smells and surroundings, and depositing it for treatment in a completely strange environment, without first blunting its fears of the transition by the use of tranquillisers.

By trial and error, unaccompanied – perhaps surprisingly – by no significant toll of casualties, we gradually found the type of sedative best suited to a particular type of patient, and, just as important, we managed to determine the appropriate dosage.

Meanwhile we had also gone on ahead with building, to our very own design, restraint boxes that would enable us to transport, and examine at close range, wild animals we could never have dared approach when they had freedom of movement in their dens.

The principle of these devices was to employ restraint by compression – the walls and roof of the box being designed in a way that enabled them to be moved either vertically or laterally, compressing the animal between them. The floor of the box was constructed of steel bars, and thus by turning the whole structure upside down it was possible to expose the animal's abdomen for intraperitoneal injection. Similarly, both roof and sides of the box were usually constructed of reinforced chain mesh, so that through the links, injections could be made into the spine or flanks, and every part of the patient exposed for examination.

The design also allowed for a remote control device that brought down a shutter, barring escape, once the animal had been lured into the box via the door of its cell.

Our boxes – restraint boxes as they became known – were astonishingly successful, and soon other zoos had enthusiastically borrowed our designs or developed their own. We also embarked on methods of restraining small mammals and birds, and drew up a programme whereby new arrivals could be acclimatised more rapidly to zoo surroundings.

This latter aim was more – far more – than a humane effort in making our animals feel welcome. In many cases a necessity, to save them from injury or death. The first six months of its life in a new environment is the testing-time for the captive animal. It is sensitive to an acute degree to change, noise and movement, and especially is it upset by the restraint imposed on it while moving it to its final accommodation.

Soon, I defined certain of our arrivals as living in what could be called, for want of a better term, a state of 'suspended stress', namely beneath an outward appearance of calm lay a condition of fear and uncertainty unparalleled in man. In this state the animal is so susceptible to fright and shock that it may succumb when apparently healthy, to circulatory failure.

Worried by the toll revealed by an investigation that we conducted into casualties among new entrants, we decided to turn once more towards the tranquillising drugs as a method of combating the patient's stress. With few exceptions, we found that this procedure enabled a newly-arrived animal to accept its new surroundings far more,

Patients Extraordinary

and with far less upset, than when it had been left with its senses unimpaired, and working towards its own destruction.

*

We were in many respects fortunate in these, the formative years of the hospital service. Never before had science made available such a multiplicity of therapeutic aids, although their application to wild animals had scarcely been considered. The psycho-therapeutic drugs – their loose definition as 'tranquillisers' stemming from the word's association with peace of mind – modified the temperament of the patient by their action on the central nervous system, and were invaluable for the premedication of most mammals before anaesthesia. But there were of course limitations to their employment, and animals on whom their use could be harmful.

Man, as a patient, can be kept in bed after an operation, but a wild animal can not. Thus it is essential in the immediate post-operative period that it should feel itself to be in full possession of its balance – if only to avoid destroying its sense of security. On slender-limbed species such as the giraffe and the gazelle tranquillisation can induce a state of stupor which may result in its swaying on its feet and perhaps losing its sense of direction. This inco-ordination we discovered could lead to serious consequences, including self-injury and fractures to the limb bone, and so we had to preclude its administration from these types of animal.

However, in general we could feel extremely fortunate in working in an age when resources were available that we could test and adapt to the needs of the animals.

Equally we were fortunate, as the years went by and knowledge of our efforts got abroad, in obtaining the enthusiastic support of several leading practitioners of human medicine and surgery, and the quiet, unofficial cooperation from some of our best-known hospitals.

Exemplifying a reasonably lighthearted, but nevertheless sophisticated, example of this form of cooperation, was the case of the toucan that lost its Beak.

This arose after the new hospital had been established, and our veterinary service, hitherto confined to Zoo animals, had been broadened to include non-domestic animal pets referred for consultation to us by local veterinary surgeons.

A male Toucan, owned by a well-respected ornithologist, had attempted to make amorous advances to a hen bird by passing his beak through the wire netting that divided their two cages. Unfortunately his reception was anything but favourable, and he had to leave a good part of the offending proboscis behind him. The female had bitten it off!

When the victim, extremely chastened, was brought to our out-patients' clinic, I had to confess at once that his injury was too complicated for us at the Zoo to handle on our own. We must look outside for expert help.

The longer beak – essential when it came to picking up food – had been completely severed, and although the bird's owner was feeding it by hand, the sense of his security occasioned by its loss was sufficient in itself to kill it. There was only one way to save our patient. We decided he must be given a new beak.

But how this could be achieved completely perplexed us. I turned to dental colleagues, and was rewarded by the promptly offered assistance of one of Britain's most eminent prosthetic dental surgeons, and his team.

Pieces of the beak were collected, and were then matched, jigsaw-style, with what remained of the original. Detailed

Patients Extraordinary

drawings were made, and plastic moulds constructed, to which was fitted an alloy frame and plastic skin, the whole being shaped to match the exact contours of the proboscis. By the time the new structure was locked on the patient, by a generous mixture of dental cement, we found it indistinguishable from the original. But how would it feel to the toucan . . . ?

It is pleasant to be able to record that the result of this meticulous effort, devoted as it was to a project that had never before been attempted, was practically and artistically perfect. Our toucan's 'false set' was even coloured to match its original – after all, we did not want the bird to be looked on by his fellows as an oddity!

To enhance the toucan's enthusiastic reception of this original piece of dental engineering, was the fact that the metal ridge we had used to reinforce the new beak developed a razor-sharpness in the weeks that followed, and although this was one development we certainly hadn't planned for, he went through the mesh to the bird next door as if equipped with wire-cutters!

Like so many other operations that appear to have no very great practical purpose, and stem in the first place from the specialist's sense of sympathy spiced by challenge presented to one's skill and imagination, the toucan affair yielded an unexpected bonus of knowledge.

Bone and beak alike had been sliced off by the female's bite, and as far as we knew, it was impossible for severed bone to grow again. There had been no real way of checking this assumption, as birds as badly injured as the toucan usually died, but it was one in such general currency that we had not thought of querying it.

Thus, on visiting our former patient later in the year, we were astonished to observe that the bone was growing

First Catch Your Tiger

again. It was not long before the toucan was able to discard its false beak and proudly flaunt its own.

*

From time to time our treatment of outside patients was performed when we were 'outside' too: notably when we were called upon to round up wild animals that had escaped from other private zoos or private owners. In some respects these incidents were more trouble than they were worth: on the other hand, there were occasions when, I suppose, the opportunity to tackle somebody else's headache in the open air and far from the hospital's day to day environment, provided us with food for experience.

One incident of this type, widely circularised in the press, was when we were asked if we could help capture Nikki and Valentin, two Russian bears that had escaped from private ownership on the Isle of Wight.

The two bears had been at liberty for two or three weeks before our services were called upon. Well-meaning local people, and animal welfare organisations that really ought to have known better, had left food and drink outside their houses and at various vantage points on the island, and, as a result of this these comparatively domesticated animals, instead of returning home for nourishment, had stayed out and had begun to resort to the wild.

It was in January that a note of urgency was suddenly injected into this peculiar situation. The bears had been seen at Nodes Point, on the sloping cliff adjacent to a holiday camp. Sightseers began to throng there in their hundreds. The situation was potentially dangerous.

Wiser than I in anticipating the attraction that the story would have for Fleet Street, Tony Dale, the Zoo's Press Relations Officer, had accompanied me from the mainland,

Patients Extraordinary

and both of us urged on our friends that – if they *must* join in the hunt – they should at all costs keep behind me.

I was armed with a Cap-chur pistol, a weapon fired by compressed CO_2 and using for ammunition a metal syringe barrel which carried an explosive charge behind its plunger. This detonated as the syringe-missile made its impact on the target, forcing the plunger down the barrel and pushing before it the liquid drug, injecting it into the animal. The dosage was sufficient to render our quarry unconscious, and would certainly kill a human, even a hardened reporter! 'So please keep behind us,' Tony and I reiterated, though we hadn't much confidence in our pleas being heeded.

There is no species more dedicated than a keen pressman on a story. As I loaded the pistol, the cameramen pressed fearlessly around me. When we set out for the chase I was flanked by volunteer 'beaters.'

We encountered the two fugitives at the foot of the cliffs, only a few yards from where they had originally been reported. They were big bears – bigger than we had expected – and it was obvious that, despite their deceptively cuddly appearance, they were capable of inflicting some very nasty damage. But this did not deter the hardy souls around me. As soon as the bears were sighted there was a massive surge forward.

Momentarily I succumbed to peevishness, but then, just as I was about to yell at the crowd to keep out of the line of fire, my foot slipped on a mound of seaweed and I fell to the ground. The pistol, which detonated, shot the dart with its lethal capsule into space.

'That's done it,' I thought, 'I've killed someone!'

The dart *must* have hit someone, I was terribly sure of that, it couldn't *not* have hit someone! I despaired. And yet, incredibly, it hadn't! It ricocheted off a rock. Again, it didn't

First Catch Your Tiger

appear that my mishap had been noticed – or at least that it had not been fully comprehended. The Cap-chur gun emits no tell-tale report, and the whoosh of the missile had happily passed unheard in the general excitement.

Fortunately for my peace of mind there were no further complications. Both bears were darted from close-range, and the drug was so fast in its action that the second of the animals to fall collapsed without even realising that its colleague had preceded him.

I went up to the casualties and examined them. They were thoroughly sedated, and would remain so for hours. There remained only the problem of getting them back home. Before we could get them to the transport truck we would have to arrange for their journey up the steeply shelving cliff.

In the end we settled for the time-honoured jungle method of slinging the captives by rope from a couple of saplings, which were then carried on the shoulders of the burliest of our 'volunteers.'

After this triumphal journey – a cross between a carnival and a return from safari – and the subsequent reception of the animals at a nearby zoo I felt that a little relaxation was appropriate, and decided that we would drop in on my mother-in-law in Esher on the way home.

'What a nice surprise to see you,' she exclaimed delightedly, promptly producing her pet Pomeranian 'Winkie.' 'I wonder, dear, if you'd cut my Winkie's nails!'

A veterinary officer can never complain that the calls made upon him lack variety.

While the Isle of Wight 'safari' predictably made the headlines, a far less well-attended bear hunt, right on my own doorstep, was conducted without the benefit of press

Patients Extraordinary

coverage: in fact publicity would have been most unwelcome at the time, escapes not being considered as enhancing the visitor-appeal of London Zoo.

In this rather fearsome incident there was to be no Capchur gun available, and I was to be involved in a free for all at a range that was far too close for comfort, and for safety too.

6. Tooth and Claw

It was late on a summer's evening. The last of our visitors had drifted home and the Zoo was quiet. I was in an armchair in my flat, relaxed and peaceful: then the telephone rang.

From the far end of the line came the voice of the Zoo's housekeeper, the imperturbable and wholly admirable Hanson. In tones so reverential that he might have been offering a visiting bishop a cup of tea, he said: 'Excuse me sir, I don't want to disturb you. But there is a beast at large in the Gardens!'

So much for peace!

I jumped into my grey Daimler and drove to the area that Hanson had indicated, around the Monkey House, but I could see no beast, except for those in the cages. The Gardens were very still. It was a warm and pleasant evening and wherever I looked, the scene was one of tranquillity. I made yet another circuit, still could see nothing, and then, a little exasperated at this disturbance to my leisure-hours, decided to leave the car and investigate on foot. It was an incredibly stupid thing to have done; especially in view of my oft repeated insistence on the need for circumspection where wild animals were concerned.

The threat of an escape had long lain heavily on me, and I had introduced precautions against such an event. Yet now I had offended against the routine's most elementary principle: namely, on your own, you don't leave the protection afforded by a car. You don't even attempt to match your speed with that of a wild animal, I had insisted, or trust to human vigilance to defeat its instinctive cunning. Yet now, after a period that had been completely accident-free, my guard had dropped and I was walking like a babe into a trap.

I walked along the length of the Monkey House from east to west, and then turned round to face the main gate. No life stirred along the broad avenues, and I decided to have a look behind the House. And then, as I did so, I came face to face with Hanson's 'beast' – and *what* a beast it was! A huge bear, in a very ugly mood – and only some six yards away!

Too late now to get back to the car. Frantically I grabbed at the only weapon available, a garden broom that had been propped against the wall.

The bear growled, threw out its great arms and came lumbering down on me. And then, looking larger than life, it reared itself on its hind legs to strike.

All my sophistication vanished. The veneer of civilisation and education cracked wide open. Reverting to the primitive, intent only on self-survival, I raised the broom and got in the first blow – a stroke to the animal's head.

Momentarily it recoiled, then came at me again, roaring and snorting, looking vast, and I hit it twice more. Then, with my foe now far too close I did the only thing that was practical to do. I ran.

Strangely, the animal did not try to pursue me, but I didn't bother at the time to check whether it had or hadn't. I knew what a bear could do with its feet and claws and teeth, and was anxious only to get out of its murderous reach. Breathless, and terribly shaken, I managed to reach my car and drove to the Keepers' Lodge, where I collected reinforcements, two keepers on emergency watch.

First Catch Your Tiger

One of my earliest actions in the Zoo had been to try and ward against the escape contingency, and to that end we had positioned nets in canisters at various key positions in the Gardens. For this precaution, I was now to be duly grateful.

Terrified though I was, I knew that we must conform to the long-established Zoo tradition of taking local risks whatever their consequences, in order to prevent an escapee leaving the Gardens and loosing itself on the public. So equipping ourselves with a net we left the friendly lodge behind us, and advanced, none too eagerly, on the Monkey House.

We came across the bear in pretty well the same spot as I had left it. As soon as it saw us it accepted the challenge, and attacked!

A minute or so later, its roars of fury raising echoes of alarm from the awakened Zoo, it was caught up in the net, and using head and claws to break through the mesh that encased its entire length; but every effort it made served only to entangle it still further. Finally, completely exhausted, its fury at last subsided, and we were able between us to hustle it back into its den.

I returned to my flat considerably wiser: for an evening off it had all been extremely noisy, but it had driven home to me the truth of the lessons I'd preached to others: to enjoy a long life it is necessary never to drop your guard.

However valuable a zoo animal may be – even if its worth is measured in five figures – and however devoted its keepers may be to it, the safety of the public takes priority in the – very rare – event of an escape. Tranquillising guns, capture nets, traps and restraint boxes . . . if it is possible by such devices to take the animal alive then so much the better, but otherwise a decision must be made that, however tragic in its impact on zoo society, is in line with the simple principle: 'The safety of the public must come first.' Such was the factor that decided the fate of Cholmondeley the Runaway Chimp.

Cholmondeley was a chimp of considerable taste and bonhomie, and enjoyed the minor vices and refinements of man, which he acquired with no undue effort. He got through twenty cigarettes a day, enjoyed the odd bottle of stout and had kept his former master company at table. He wore clothes like any human and had manners that were better than some. Unfortunately for Cholmondeley, however, the imprint of man had made a deeper impression on him than even these surface appearances served to indicate. The chimpanzee, who otherwise would have been leading an uncomplicated life among the trees, had been captured as an infant, and over the years had almost ceased to identify with his species.

It was only when his master had to retire and found himself unable to keep him in domestic surroundings, that Cholmondeley began to experience the disadvantages of his state. He was presented to the Zoo to look after, and truly hated the change. Little by little the chimpanzee's once happy spirit flagged and he became morose and sorely troubled. His health began to suffer, and he showed signs of variable temper. But really, what else could one expect?

In Cholmondeley we had a classic example of what can happen to an animal that, brought out of its natural habitat, is taught so assiduously to imitate the human and acquire his trappings that he eventually accepts the role imposed upon him as natural to him, and loses all memory of his primitive past.

In such circumstances, it is easy to imagine the bewilderment – and sense of indignity – experienced by the chimp

First Catch Your Tiger

when stripped of his clothes and confined to the company of his far less sophisticated brethren. And the routine of life in the den – pleasant though it might be to the average inmate – must have been deadly boring to one who had, in his time, been so high on the social ladder.

I have always held that a zoo environment, provided that its standards approximated to those maintained by London, is preferable for most creatures to the hazards of an existence in the jungle, but there are exceptions, and Cholmondeley was one of them.

As the weeks went by it became obvious to us that Cholmondeley was the victim of a developing psychosis. At times he was subject to the most violent fits of passion and rage, but mostly he would sit unstirring in his den, refusing all food and drink, and resistant to all attempts to dissipate his gloom. But one day he developed a new behaviour trait: his keeper found him stroking and squeezing his face, groaning and grimacing as he did so.

Called in to observe this latest manifestation of the animal's misery, I felt that it was caused by physical pain, very probably toothache, and decided to examine him, under anaesthesia of course.

In those days, the only effective method of anaesthetising an animal of Cholmondeley's size and type was provided by a primitive form of gas chamber, a box into which chloroform was piped through an inlet in the side. But although we managed to lure our patient into this device, he was by no means cooperative in the period that followed.

We turned on the gas, and waited for him to lapse into unconsciousness and then waited some more, for nothing appeared to be happening! The chimp was still on his feet, and apparently unconcerned. Several more minutes passed, and still he failed to succumb: it seemed that the gas was having no effect at all. Taking a puzzled look at Cholmondeley, I found him staring back at me with some aplomb. With one hairy paw resting against the side of the box, and the other reflectively scratching his massive chest, he looked more at ease than he had been for months past, and this only added to my bewilderment. Here, so it seemed, was a rare phenomenon, one that made mock of all our past experience.

It was only when one of the team passed to the far side of the chimp, and suddenly burst out laughing, that we realised the reason for the chimp's extraordinary resistance. Cholmondeley's paw was being used for more than a prop – he had placed his index finger neatly over the mouth of the gas-pipe!

Unfortunately this incident was to be the very last example, bar one, of the intelligence and resource of this most remarkable animal, and the tricks that had once earned him a seat at the Captain's Table . . .

Cholmondeley's quarters in the 'Sanny' had a door that – because of its age and vulnerability – had been strengthened by steel. This, he took quite literally in his stride! He left his den by the simple expedient of lifting the door frame from the ancient brickwork. Minutes later, I got the warning 'Chimp At Large.' Of all the confused attempts to save Cholmondeley from the consequences of his action, the one most near to success – and certainly the bravest – was that made by Bill Harwood, a Zoo official of long service and experience, and involved in so many of the Zoo's activities that it was sometimes difficult to see where his responsibilities began and ended.

Bill behaved like a hero in the Cholmondeley affair. Regardless of risk, he gave chase to the angry chimp, caught up with him and, very sensibly, pressed on him a

First Catch Your Tiger

bottle of stout. Then with supreme effrontery, and an incredible feat of persuasion, he somehow got him to sit down, and join him in yet another pint.

For a moment, it looked as though Bill's plan to detain the animal until help arrived to get him back to his den was going to work. But then, as if sensing the net that was closing round him, Cholmondeley jumped angrily to his feet, and made off again, more furious than ever. He was now beyond all efforts of salvation.

The chimp had reached Gloucester Gate before our attempts at *rapprochement* were forced to a grinding halt. With dense traffic in the road outside, and scores of unsuspecting citizens enjoying the sunshine in the park, there was no degree of tolerance left for the unfortunate animal.

The Society's 'Butcher', whose deadly accurate marksmanship was reserved for those few grim occasions when all soft options had failed, was reluctantly called upon, and arrived with rifle in hand.

He used just one bullet to despatch Cholmondeley – the chimp who, without wanting to, had become a menace to the species he had been taught to regard as his own; and, as we looked at the crumpled body, I don't think there was one of us that did not feel a sense of guilt. When one remembered the way in which the animal had been 'humanised' the incident smacked almost of fratricide and I shall always look back on it as one of the most painful things to have happened during my career at the Zoo. But, for all that, it is true to say that however well-loved a zoo animal may be, the safety of humans just *has* to come first.

While Cholmondeley's escape, and subsequent fate, attracted considerable attention, another escape, which could have had far more serious consequences, was completely unknown to the press or visitors to the Zoo. Yet this occurred on a day when the Gardens were crowded and the animals concerned in it were separated from the innocent public by only a matter of yards, and, as it transpired, the authority of the keeper.

My own involvement in this affair arose because, in the course of my rounds, I paused to chat with some of the keepers in the Lion House. We were in the Men's Mess at the time, and overlooked from where we stood the entire length of the aisle that divided the animals' sleeping dens from the front cages in which they could be viewed by the public. To allow the lions to move from den to cage, a series of overhead bridges with plank floors and walls of iron bars spanned the aisles, and these too came within our line of vision. The House was impressive in size – and certainly steeped in antiquity, a place of dark brick and heavy shadows.

I had momentarily turned my back on it, when one of my companions cut into what I was saying with a shout of sheer incredulity and alarm. Wheeling round, I followed the direction of his gaze . . . to see part of the floor of one of the bridges collapse into the aisle. A moment later a lion and lioness fell through the gap, and then, recovering themselves, started to stalk towards the exit!

To say that we were horrified would have been an understatement; for the moment we could hardly believe what we were seeing. Then the full peril posed by the incident hit us. In a few seconds the lions would reach the end of the aisle, and get out among the crowd of happy visitors!

So what should be done? I was completely lost for an answer. I could do nothing to stop these animals – not stop them in time. And neither, it occurred to me, could anyone else.

First Catch Your Tiger

It was then, however, that my opinion was confounded by a keeper running past me and towards his charges. 'Get back,' he bellowed at them. 'You bloody well get back to your den!'

The lions paused, and turned on him their perpetually worried gaze. 'Get back,' repeated the keeper, waving a clenched fist. 'You heard what I said – you bloody well get back to your den!'

The male began to swish his tail, the female crouched beside him, and then, to our amazement, the tension of the pair relaxed, and, one behind the other, they leaped guiltily back on to the bridge. A moment later they had passed through the gap, and doubled back to whence they came.

In the private 'inquest' that followed, it transpired that the structure of the bridge was so old that it was almost completely rotted. Needless to say, the work of restoration was very prompt, and very thorough.

*

It takes all sorts of animals to make up a zoo, and by that I do not necessarily mean to stress the glaringly obvious. Animals, like humans, do not vary only in respect of their species: their characters too, are widely varied. So are their responses to man and his environment.

But for an animal that is almost invariably vicious, there is no equal to that favourite of zoo visitors, the 'pretty' little zebra!

A zebra is the only animal I know of that can leap with all four feet off the ground and bite and kick you before it touches the floor again. A zebra *wills* its body to kill you, even when it is at the end of its tether, and can employ for that purpose a head as hard as a hammer and hooves of iron.

Not many people are aware of the Jekyll and Hyde

propensities of the zebra, or the strength and malice it can deploy when angry or frightened. For that matter, I too was in happy ignorance of it until I operated on a zebra mare.

To keep that patient safe from interruption in the critical phase when it was recovering from its anaesthetic, I removed her mate from the den, and transferred him to quarters elsewhere. He didn't like the idea at all, and soon began to make his feelings known.

That night, the sound of the stallion's fury echoed over the Gardens, and was heard even by us in the flat – an awful commotion, the outcry of a killer. At last it got so bad that I could stand it no longer, and ignoring all family protests, grabbed a torch and went out to see if I could do anything to quieten the animal.

What a hope! As I approached the Zebra House, the stallion's frenzy reached its peak, and the door was set trembling beneath the angry impact of its body.

It was very late, and no help was to hand. I was awed by the zebra's display of strength and rage, but I was also worried about its safety – and my own. Let it stay where it was, and it ran the risk of battering itself to death. Let it out and I could be trampled beneath its initial onrush. So what to do?

Had I known then what I know now about the habits of the zebra, and what the animal will do when enraged or frightened, it is possible that my answer might have been other than the one I eventually made. Even as it was, I had little stomach for my task.

As I stood in front of the Zebra House, with my hand on the latch, my ears were almost numbed by the squeals of rage, and the hoof-blows on the door, and I fearfully decided to let it be, and go back home to bed. But no sooner had the move been formulated than conscience

First Catch Your Tiger

intervened, and made a fool of caution. I waited just long enough to let the stallion reach the furthermost end of its den, and then I lifted the latch – and ran!

I am still at a loss to know how I reached the gate, with the stallion's hot breath drenching the back of my neck; but somehow I *did* reach it, and got through, and managed to shut it behind me. As I did so the hooves of the zebra lashed out, and smashed against the barrier, splintering it. Then, whinnying madly, my opponent attacked again, while I looked on, quite appalled, at the menace from which I had so narrowly escaped.

Next morning, I encountered a group of keepers talking together outside the Zebra House.

'How did the zebra get out?' they asked me.

'I let him out. I went in and opened the gate!'

They looked at me with expressions of awe and pity combined.

'He's a killer,' said one of them flatly.

'He wasn't exactly amicable,' I conceded. 'But he seems to have quietened down now.'

The stallion was standing perfectly still, with his back towards us and looking the very picture of docility, but the keeper was unimpressed.

Without a word, he took out a thin cigarette paper and, gesturing me to watch, edged it just a fraction through the bars.

There was a sound like a gun exploding. The zebra had used only one hind leg, but the cigarette paper had been split in two!

'Yes, he's a real killer,' said the keeper, before adding with some concern, 'Are you all right, sir? You've gone quite white!'

7. When Sabre's Heart Stopped Beating

From the tips of his shapely paws to the crown of his velvet-smooth head, Sabre the Puma was an animal of dramatic beauty. His walk was a rhythmic swagger, his whiskers were cavalier, and his every action proclaimed the noble savage. But the most striking of all his physical attributes was his calculating arrogant gaze. Cool and yellow, his oriental eyes surveyed you through the silky fringe of their long lashes, sizing you up and down, stripping you of pretensions. If ever there was a 'cool cat' it was Sabre!

He had come to us from an unexpected source – the Royal Canadian Air Force. There he had served as mascot to the Cougar Squadron – cougar being the North American variant of the family name – until his owners had gone home, trusting him to the Zoo's care in the early 'fifties.

At the time of which I write, Sabre was over thirteen years old but was as active, and as resilient, as a cub – though certainly without a cub's frivolity. Weighing 260 pounds, he had one of the cleanest health records in the Zoo. His skin seemed to glow with health and vitality.

And then, quite unexpectedly, something happened to shatter the confident calm of this aloof aristocrat. His keeper reported that he was showing signs of stress, and appeared to have some sort of wound on his flank. After a look at Sabre we came to the conclusion that he had

First Catch Your Tiger

developed a deep tissue ulcer, and was aggravating it by persistent licking.

In a man such a condition would have been easily treated and cured; as a minor affliction quickly terminated. With an animal patient the process is far more complex. One cannot swathe a puma in bandages, or smooth healing ointments over its smarting wound. In fact, one can do very little, without sustaining damage. A sick wild animal is a very poor patient. And anyone who approaches it too closely is – as a security risk – poorer still. Slight though the trouble might be, we had, therefore, no option but to put in hand the same sort of extensive programme – involving restraint and anaesthesia – as would have applied to the most major, and most complicated, of operations.

One of the most frustrating, and least appreciated, aspects of operating on a wild animal is the amount of time and effort that's absorbed before you can even bring it to the table.

As the patient can't possibly explain to you how it feels – and as *you* can't explain to *it* the various steps you intend to take for its relief! – you have to implement a programme that involves a whole series of separate manoeuvres (each of them vital), and demands an expenditure of resources and time that often may seem disproportionate to the scale of the medical problem proper. Sabre's case is no exception to the rule.

To move our puma into hospital without incident or injury, we have first to tranquilise and box him. Next, on the night before the operation, we have to administer sedation in order to prevent his being disturbed by the unfamiliar surroundings, and thus be in danger of losing confidence and, with it, his natural resistance. And next, on the morning of the day itself, we have to tranquillise him yet again, for his trip to the operating table.

This entails his being transferred to the specially constructed restraint box, and, once this is done, we are able to reach through the bars that form its sides and restrain his paw, injecting him with a light surgical anaesthetic. Thoroughly drowsy, our patient is removed from the box, lifted on to the stretcher, carried to the table and secured there. The critical stage of the pre-operational programme is now complete.

There are, however, further things to be done before we can commence the operation itself, and the team performs the functions with the smoothness that comes of practice.

An endotracheal tube is inserted into the trachea, and the pneumatic cuff it carries is inflated while connection is made with the circuit anaesthetic machine, to maintain anaesthesia.

Next we open the tapes, and fit the drip into the puma's leg before turning to the site, which must be clipped and shaved, and made secure against infection. And then we change into sterilised clothing, fit our masks, and apply sterile surgical drapes to the patient.

We do these things at speed, for time is not our ally. The animal has to be kept anaesthetised, to a degree that will protect the team from being attacked by their patient. But the anaesthesia must not be so deep as to interfere with the pace of his subsequent recovery, and constantly the gas mixture has to be adjusted.

When we inspect the ulcer we find it is quite a monster. It is three inches wide, and copiously suppurating, but we foresee little difficulty in the task of removing it. Sabre appears to be comfortable – 'out to the world' as they say –

First Catch Your Tiger

and, of course, the operation is a purely routine affair. But then something happens that is completely unexpected. A cardiac arrest. The patient's heart has stopped beating!

Produced for the cinema, the moment would have been one that was 'drenched in drama.' In real-life things tend to wear a somewhat sober aspect. The drama is there, but you are not conscious of it. You're far too busy trying to calculate the next move, and clutched with terror at the possibility of losing the patient.

On this occasion, reaction stemmed from the subconscious, and was sharp. Swiftly I injected the animal's heart with adrenalin, and then commenced external massage – a vigorous thumbing rib massage – to stimulate the motionless heart. Half a minute later, it had resumed its natural beat, and we could start again, the position stabilised.

By chance, at the Zoo's invitation, there were in the theatre at the time one of Fleet Street's most respected cameramen, Freddie Reed of the *Daily Mirror*, and his reporter colleague, Betty Tay, who specialised – and still does – in stories about animals, of which she has an encyclopaedic knowledge.

The Society had given them what was, in those days, the rare opportunity of recording a Zoo operation, and – thanks to their wide experience – neither was of the type to sensationalise what they saw. However, even Miss Tay was sufficiently impressed by the occasion subsequently to record: 'I watched as they massaged the animal's heart for thirty seconds. It seemed to me more like thirty minutes!'

I, personally, did not find it so.

The layman has time to use his imagination, and thus feels to the full the emotional impact of a crisis. But the surgeon is limited in his approach to the pure mechanics of

When Sabre's Heart Stopped Beating

the matter, and reacts automatically to their demands. The crisis over, the team changed into new sterile gowns and, within minutes of Sabre's assisted return from his brush with death, the ulcer had been removed and we had started to suture healthy skin over the surface of the wound.

Only when the puma was being wheeled out of the theatre and into the hospital's convalescent ward, did I realise that my face was running with sweat.

*

Some call it stoicism... to others it's 'the stiff upper lip'... but the capacity of some men to grin in the face of disaster and say, even against all reason, 'I am going to get better,' springs from a conscious and perhaps sub-conscious summing-up of a critical situation, which is accompanied by the desire to do something about it, and seek a remedy. No such sophistication is possessed by the wild animal. Should he fall sick when in his natural habitat the chances are that he will die.

He will die because he is no longer fit enough to hunt for food, or because his illness will have left him easy prey for the predators. He will die because his own kind will destroy him, regarding him as a burden on the herd or group, endangering their own safety. Or else – as if he were aware of these things – he will die from the fear of them. A sick man can look to friends or relatives, or even to the Government, for sympathy and support. A sick wild animal can turn to no one but itself. No animal feels 'sympathy' for another. The sick animal is everyone's enemy – and he knows it. Accordingly he is vulnerable.

We know what powerful physiological, mental and emotional responses can be summoned up from even the weakest of human bodies. Few of these aids are mobilised by the animal. If he manages to survive the preliminary stages of his illness we may say of him, as we may do of a human, that he has achieved the will to live. If he fails to survive, when the medical odds appear to have been in his favour, then in nine cases out of ten it is because, in his fear he has seemingly negated this will to live. He has replaced it, albeit unconsciously, with what may be termed 'the will to die!'

Fear is a great killer. It can slay the clever human, let alone the animal. Thus fear of 'magic' will cause a primitive to creep away into the bush and die, while fear of a simple jab from a hypodermic has poleaxed many a contemporary Westerner. Man has talked much of fear, and confidently defined its causes and effects. He has given it a philosophy, and 'explained' it in terms of reason. With such phrases as 'adrenal exhaustion,' 'powers of suggestion,' 'stress syndrome' and so forth, he has boldly rationalised it – and then he has turned, for reassurance against its impact, to religion and the resources of psychiatry. But the animal has no such assistance in times of trouble, and it is stupid for humans to think that his defences can be strengthened by the administration of a medicinal regime. A doctor gains much of his success, when dealing with man, from the fact that he is a symbol of recovery. He is important for what he *is*; not merely for what he *does*. A wild animal cannot appreciate the image!

Discordancies in its environment, the imposition of medical programmes, even a taste or smell that strikes it as unpleasant – each of these is sufficient in itself to aggravate an animal's natural capacity for alarm, and ignite the explosive forces that lie within it, nearly all of them destructive. With the animal 'the will to die' is perhaps no mere figure of speech, employed to cover a failure of modern medicine, but a psychological factor that can govern its physical fate.

Although the major victim of the fear psychosis is the animal in the wild, its contemporary in the zoo is almost equally vulnerable. When beset by pressures with which it is ill-equipped to deal, the animal surrenders. In modern parlance it 'opts out;' rather than try and cope with its dilemma it drifts into the line of least resistance. In short, the animal acquires the will to die, and most assuredly *will* die – unless there is intervention from outside, to impose a method of rescue.

A basic ingredient to any attempt at rescue or cure, was to remove the patient from the circumstances or situation that it found unacceptable, and substitute for them factors that it would find more acceptable. To make this technique effective, however, the animal nursing attendant, with his day to day experience of a particular animal's whims and fancies, appeared initially to be a far more useful person than the veterinary surgeon, and therefore I had emphasised that the veterinary surgeon with his instinctive desire to intervene with every weapon in his armoury, was to be called upon only in the last resort, when the animal's emotional status had been stabilised and medication or surgery could be of meaningful significance.

Quiet, warmth, semi-darkness, a selection of pleasant foods – accompanied by a switch from the environment it associated with the onset of its illness; the provision of these things could do far more for the animal during its preliminary depression than ever I could with my professional techniques. With luck, they could even tilt the balance of the procedure that carried the patient's resistance down the path that leads to death, and convert it into the sort of reaction that results in health and fitness.

Nursing has an entirely different connotation when applied to the wild animal than when it has when experienced by the domestic animal and man. The latter's concept of nursing is a programme – or discipline if you like – of medication and administration. It is accompanied by a cycle of sheet-changing, bed-bathing, the taking of temperatures. Bed pans and matron's rounds do not impress the tiger or the wolf!

If it is to be successful, the nursing of wild animals must give first priority to the creation of a tranquil atmosphere, free of trauma and shock, and the provision of warmth by irradiation, and for example the administration of oxygen where necessary. A special diet should also be arranged, but it should be made up of dishes the patient fancies rather than be forced on it in the belief that it 'does it good.' And certainly the last thing an animal will require at *this* stage of its illness will be forcefully administered medicine or drugs.

Attempts to administer such 'aids' by mixing them with the patient's food or drinking water are almost certainly doomed to failure, and can even do positive harm. A wild animal's senses are many times more acute than those of the domestic pet, and infinitely more so than man's.

Medication is completely foreign to a wild animal, and it will detect – and reject – any attempt to impose it. Worse, it will positively rebel against it, and thus add to the extent of its emotional upset.

It was in the light of such circumstances that we decided that, except in cases of the odd exception where specific emergency action – such as surgery, oxygen therapy, or fluid replacement therapy – was immediately required, it was best to leave a patient to his own devices for the first twenty-four hours of his illness. Given intolerable conditions the animal could then balance its physiology – or so we reasoned – and this would be the prerequisite to any attempt to apply medical techniques to the task of achieving its relief.

By providing the animal with facilities for isolation and nomadic living – withdrawn from the particular stimuli that had created its stresses and tension – we at the Zoo hospital did our best to enable it to withstand the fears and shock induced by its initial sickness, and allowed it to develop its strength and confidence for the time when more drastic action might be required. Spontaneous recoveries on many occasions well illustrate the point. Would this – could this – happen to man?

*

Blind, unreasoning, instinctive and utterly primitive, an animal's fears can not only result in its literally 'frightening itself to death', it can also lead to the destruction of its young.

Many a mammal will devour its cubs in order to remove all traces of their existence from a potential aggressor. It will do this because of its sense of insecurity, and it would appear that the purpose of its action is to protect not only itself, and the rest of the herd, but also – by some freak of instinct – to 'protect' the very offspring it destroys.

In other cases, fear of the presence of an enemy will result in dead litters, and mental and physical illness for the mother.

One of my earliest encounters with this sort of tragedy took place when a pregnant female puma fell ill, and it was decided to carry out a Caesarean section.

The plight of the puma had puzzled us for quite a while previously. Every one of her previous cubs had been delivered dead and we were completely at a loss to know

First Catch Your Tiger

why. New, at that time, to the vagaries and complexities of animal psychology, and turning to the textbook for guidance – and not finding any – we were far too naïve to appreciate the clue provided by the positioning of the animal's living and sleeping quarters. It was too close to the public – far too close!

Many animals will normally lie up in isolation as their time of parturition labour draws near, and this trait is particularly marked in the case of the sensitive 'cats,' of whom our puma was a fairly typical example.

In mammalian parturition the stages are basically threefold. There is stage one, the contraction of the uterus (labour pains), stage two including abdominal contractions, the delivery, and the expulsion of the foetal membranes as stage three.

Among animals the point where real problems – indeed danger – can arise lies between the end of stage one and the beginning of stage two. If at that moment – when the uterus has contracted, but the baby has not been delivered – there is serious interruption to the emotional stability of the mother, then there is the likelihood of secondary uterine inertia. All systems stop.

Because at this stage the delivery is so much dependent on the mother, this means an almost certain death for the baby who may no longer be being nourished from the womb and the possibility of disease for its parent. Such was the case with our puma.

It was the proximity of the crowd that had frightened her, and shaken her from her emotional balance. In the wild, an animal has its young in conditions of near secrecy, thus indulging its protective instinct. Noise can mean enemies, and a menace to mother and child. Thus our puma had panicked when denied the environment that, throughout the entire history of its species, had been essential to breeding. But we weren't to know that.

After considerable thought we decided that the only way to solve the mystery of the puma's overdue pregnancy and generally worried condition, was to conduct a Caesarean section. When we did so, we found three dead cubs inside our patient, and then we had to cope with the subsequent sepsis.

It appeared that the puma's cervix had dilated, ready to discharge her babies, but then she had stopped her contractions, and thus had allowed infection from her vagina, over which she regularly defecated, to rise into the uterus. Pus had formed there, and foetal death had followed.

Sad though it was, however, our early experience taught us a very useful lesson, and, in the long run, had a fortunate sequel.

It was decided to send the recovered convalescent off to Whipsnade and there, in surroundings that were natural to her species, our puma became pregnant again, emerging this time as the happy mother of a very live and healthy family.

8. Tiger on the Table

While Sabre the Puma was remarkably handsome even when judged by the standards of a remarkably handsome species, Kumari the tigress gave an even greater impression of the great cats family's savage strength and apparent dignity.

Although only a year old, she was over 300 lbs in weight, and possessed not even the minimum of superfluous fat to conceal the smooth working of the muscles that sent their rhythmic ripples over her magnificent striped skin.

But now, as we stood beside the operating table, all that we could see of her was a single eye, glaring motionless and gooseberry-sized, from a sea of apple-green drapes. While the behaviour that had brought her to this plight smacked more of the ethics of the alley-cat than what one would have expected from the mate of the redoubtable Rajah.

Kumari's trouble sprang from a dispute over lunch. She had bolted her own meat, and then tried to make off with Rajah's, and the indignant male had promptly objected. He had struck her hard – a massive punch from his paw connecting with her left eye. Soon, a slight closing of the lids, coupled with a discharge, and swelling of the globe, was observed, and we suspected that serious damage might have been done.

It was decided to have Kumari transferred to the hospital for examination – a thoroughly meticulous examination that would be carried out by one of the greatest ophthalmo-

Tiger on the Table

logists of our day. I refer to the late Sir Benjamin Ryecroft, knighted for his services to research and eye surgery, and at that time the Society's Consulting Ophthalmologist.

To Sir Ben – the benefactor of many hundreds of human patients – Kumari represented a very special sort of challenge. He was to give freely of his time and skill and courage to the cause of an animal that would cheerfully have destroyed him. To us, the consideration of the procedures involved presented a most daunting prospect but at least we had the satisfaction of confronting it when in good company!

Examining the eye of a tiger at close quarters and endeavouring to obtain an accurate diagnosis, is not the simplest or least nerve-racking of procedures, and requires most of the paraphernalia – and effort – normally associated with a major operation.

In the case of Kumari, this was further complicated by the fact that one had to obtain free access not only into the surface of the eye, but must also somehow contrive to examine visually everything inside it, and this required, in the first place, sedation followed by very effective anaesthesia and dilatation of the pupil. This was essential not only for the welfare of the animal but also for the physical safety of our hospital team, and it was only after the most careful thought that we decided on a programme that, extravagant though it may seem to those accustomed to dealing with reasonable humans, we regarded as providing the maximum security that was consistent with the examination's efficiency.

On the evening before the operation Kumari was premedicated with promazine – fed to her by mouth – and this was followed by a further dose of the drug, administered intramuscularly, at 8.30 the following morning.

First Catch Your Tiger

By 10.30 our patient was relaxed and quiet, and we were able to remove her – caged in her restraint box – to the operating theatre. There she was injected with thiopentone, administered intravenously into the saphena vein of the right leg, and started to check on her reflexes.

Only when a series of tests, including the withdrawal of her tongue from the mouth, followed by tapping on the fraenum linguae, had been satisfactorily carried out, was it possible for our patient to be transferred to the operating table, and secured there so that endotracheal intubation could be conducted, and anaesthesia completed. Then – and only then – were we able to illuminate the globe of the affected eye, and discover that the injury was even more serious than we had thought.

Rajah's blow had been delivered with such force that it had ruptured the oval capsule, in which the lens is suspended between the two chambers of the eye, and had thrown the lens into the delicate membrane of the anterior chamber. The reaction to this situation was increasing pressure within the eye which was assuming the appearance of glaucoma. There was no help for it; the lens would have to come out.

Such was the prelude to an operation of great delicacy and some danger; an operation of such intricacy and difficulty that so far as is known it had never before been attempted on a wild animal. It was one that was to demand such skill and accuracy that we were once more content to play a purely secondary role.

Sir Ben, then in his fifties, was in many respects the epitome of the brilliant surgeon. An elegant figure of a man, with a quietly confident manner he brought reassurance to the most timid of human patients. To me, however, Sir Ben is

Tiger on the Table

mainly memorable as a man who, however much beset by the demands arising from his formidable reputation, always found time to encourage his juniors, and assist them whenever he could.

Thus, when he confirmed the diagnosis and offered personally to conduct the operation, it was with considerable gratitude that we accepted. It was indeed a rare opportunity that had come our way – the opportunity of watching one of the world's most eminent eye surgeons engage himself on an operation on a wild animal, and in doing so, fulfil a function that was historically unique. We fixed a date.

Our job was to 'prepare' Kumari, and so successfully anaesthetise her that, throughout the delicate procedure of opening up the eyeball and entering its cavities, no twitching or movement of any sort would occur to restrict the surgeon in his art, or divert him even momentarily from the extraction. As a task, this was a responsible and difficult one.

Among other things, it meant a particular depth of anaesthesia would have to be maintained and regularised for a long time, and this of course could not be introduced until the animal had been sedated and restrained.

However, our previous experience of Kumari – acquired during the examination – led us to believe that an intravenous injection of 0.79 grammes of promazine would be sufficient for her initial tranquillisation, and this was duly administered at 8.30 a.m. on the day of the operation. An hour later, our patient was lying peacefully in her box, showing only the most modest interest in what was going on around her, and 'registering' her apparent feelings about it all by only an occasional – and almost benign – flick of the ear, or mild movement of her head.

We then tested her reflexes, and found that her reactions

First Catch Your Tiger

to stimuli were sluggish and quite weak. Our tranquillisation had proved effective, and the time had come to proceed to the next stage.

This entailed the administration of an initial light intravenous anaesthetic, in order to render the animal unconscious during the critical transition from the security of her restraint box to the operating table. There she would be safely restrained, as a prelude to the deeper surgical anaesthetic that the operation itself would require.

To those who give no thought to the almost abysmal differences between operating on human patients and animals – the latter incapable of explaining their symptoms, and completely deaf to any explanation of what one is doing for their cure – the procedure that this move entailed would doubtless have seemed spectacular and perhaps a little over-dramatic.

It took six men to carry the outsize stretcher – with three hundred pounds of disturbingly beautiful animal overlapping its edges – and position Kumari on the operating table. Next, her right hind leg had to be shaved to accept the intravenous drip, while her massive paw hung over the side of the table like a menacing fist. And next a wooden 'gag' had to be inserted between her jaws, to prevent her accidentally closing her mouth and so biting through the endotracheal tube, which, slipped into her trachea, would carry the Fluothane, oxygen and nitrous oxide gas used during the operation.

It was not until 11.42 – three hours and 12 minutes after tranquillisation – that Kumari was deemed ready for her operation and Sir Benjamin and his team were invited into the theatre.

Sir Benjamin Ryecroft was always courteous. Necessarily

Tiger on the Table

he was equally efficient. Fearless he now had to be, and highly adaptable.

While we were acclimatised to the improvisations enforced by 'economies,' and were well-used to the vagaries, the savagery, and the crude unreasoning fears of animal patients, Sir Ben had performed like a high priest the rites of human surgery. Flanked always by willing acolytes he had conducted operations in a church-like atmosphere where – had they been present – not even the flies would have buzzed. As the surgeon entered our theatre, we were acutely conscious of the gulf between his experience and our own, and were suitably awed by its visual manifestation expressed in the shape and size of his supporting team.

Two surgical registrars, a nursing sister, a theatre nurse, and a senior anaesthetist, who acted in the role of observer – the procession was formidable indeed. But how would its members react, we wondered, to the sight of our massive and seemingly fearsome patient? We need not have worried. Sir Benjamin was operating within seven minutes of his entry.

Kumari's pupil was dilated: the globe was fixed by sutures to make sure it did not move: and then the surgeon, calm and cool as if presiding at a Moorfields demonstration, made his first incision, cutting into the corneal limbus.

But then, as we watched him start to probe for the floating lens, we were suddenly aware that he'd encountered difficulty. The lens had so far been held in the anterior chamber, but suddenly it had slipped into the posterior chamber, a deep dark void!

At that moment, too, Kumari suffered a respiratory embarrassment, and the depth of anaesthesia was increased.

To the visiting anaesthetist, this was too much to bear. Already astounded by the quantities of gas absorbed by the animal, and worried about its possible effect, he now intervened to suggest: 'Couldn't you lower it a little?'

Tongue in cheek, I obliged. Within thirty seconds there was a slight movement from the animal's club-like paw, and nothing more was heard from my colleague of the dangers of excess!

Meanwhile, Sir Benjamin had found that it was impossible even to see the lens in its new position but, undeterred, he decided to explore for it, using a Vectis loop.

By 12.10 he had located and neatly removed the lens.

Gripped in his forceps, it was caught briefly by the light, glittering like a sliver of melted glass as one observer put it: and then, without fuss, Sir Ben had turned to the final phase of his effort.

He sutured the cornea, sewed the eyelids together, and by 12.33 the operation was complete.

It had lasted in all for forty-four minutes and the preparation for it had occupied nearly three and a half hours!

It was only when Kumari, still intubated and unconscious, had been wheeled back to her den, that one of our visitors gave vent to the pent-up tensions and emotions induced by this critical operation in a completely strange environment – and passed out!

Some while later, I had the good fortune to encounter Sir Benjamin, after a meeting at the Royal Society of Medicine and he insisted with typical politeness on introducing me to his colleagues.

'I want you to meet this man,' he told them, 'because he did a very rare thing indeed. He anaesthetised a tiger for me!'

And then, generously and with a typical twinkle and a smile, he added: 'And I have to say that that tiger was kept

Tiger on the Table

more still, and was more perfectly anaesthetised than many of the human beings on whom I have operated.'

The meeting had been of anaesthetists and he was, quite typically, enjoying a kindly leg-pull.

While the intricate surgery involved in Kumari's eye operation had posed problems of restraint and anaesthesia, the vastly different plight of an even more outsize patient presented considerable difficulty as regards its diagnosis.

First hint of the affair arose when Kim, a very beautiful – but extremely formidable – lioness, began to show signs of unaccustomed stress. This was accompanied by evident dissatisfaction with her surroundings, and her keeper turned to the Hospital for advice and remedy.

Immediately we were agreed on what could be a possible explanation: Kim and her mate had been observed to be copulating frequently, and our patient might well be pregnant. But this was theory only: just how could we make sure?

With an animal whose abdomen was normally massive, the obvious answer just did not apply!

An expectant lioness seldom gives much visual evidence of her condition. Her bulk is so vast that any additional thickness is scarcely noticeable. And Kim – a giant among giants – could at any time have carried half a dozen cubs without revealing a trace of them. Even the most observant eye would have failed to have distinguished any signs of change in the shape of her body, let alone have identified the stage of her pregnancy.

A lioness defies the normal processes of clinical assessment and any close examination can be ruled out right away. At the best of times the most belligerent of females, pregnancy will turn her into a certain killer.

First Catch Your Tiger

Because of these difficulties, the first significant indication of pregnancy is usually to be found in the behavioural pattern rather than the physical shape of the animal, and this is often expressed in a tendency for it to withdraw from its everyday environment in order to 'lie up.'

The lioness is a mammal who prefers to have her young in private, and often her condition is confirmed only by the first yelps of her new-born cubs; was this, we wondered, to be the case with Kim? Or was her apparent upset attributable to a cause other than child-bearing? We just did not know. The examination of blood and urine as an aid to pregnancy diagnosis is effective enough when applied to women. It is a far less accurate guide when applied to wild animals, and the samples are a thousand times more difficult to obtain.

The positive confirmation of our suspicions was thus quite late in arriving. And when it did, it was fairly dramatic. First, her keeper observed a flow of blood from Kim's vagina. Next we discovered a dead, and very much malformed, cub. We had trouble on our hands.

It was obvious of course that *something* should be done, and done quickly, for Kim's health, and yet what could – or should – be done, eluded us. Were there any more cubs inside her? If there were, were they dead or alive? We didn't know, not for sure. There was insufficient evidence. Was our lioness herself in danger? Again, we just did not know.

In a sense, we were confronted by the classical dilemma of the surgeon when denied the analytical facts on which to assess his patient's need for treatment and plan its nature. Do you wait for more evidence, and if you do, for how long? Or do you move, and, if you do, to what? Act too precipitately, and we might destroy the mother's confidence, and perhaps seal the fate of a valuable litter. Wait too long, and the animal could be lost to us for ever.

After careful thought we felt that, in the long run, delay could be more dangerous than action. Regardless of the fact that we had no accurate clinical analysis of the animal's state, we decided we had no option but to operate. If Kim's labour had stopped during second stage there would be all the problems associated with uterine inertia. There might also be the hazard of sepsis to be coped with. We must find out what was wrong – which meant that we must enter the abdomen surgically.

We decided to conduct an exploratory laparotomy.

The description of Kim as 'a giant among giants' did not seem overdrawn as the lioness was brought into the operating theatre and laid on the table, which she overlapped in all directions.

Similarly the problems of the operation itself assumed over-size dimensions and by the time our preliminary measures were complete, and the huge area around the site had been shaved, cleansed, and draped in sterile drapes, two hours had gone by. Having scrubbed up and gowned, I then had to make a dummy incision to mark the exact spot where I would incise into the abdomen.

Using the back of the scalpel, I first marked a 'North to South' incision on the skin down the flank, and then made a series of markings that ran crossways all the way down. This was essential as a guide to suturing the wound when the exploration had been completed, as only the most meticulous accuracy would prevent irritation or pain; which pain could entail the removal of the sutures by the patient. Any stress caused by inefficient suturing will make the animal frightened and angry, and it will seek to eliminate, by attack, the 'source' of its trouble: one just can not tell an animal patient to leave his wound alone!

Again unlike a human patient, an animal is not going to spend a period in bed, recovering slowly from its operation. It must be on its feet, and feeling fit within hours of its emergence from the effects of the anaesthetic. If it is not – if its instant return to normality is hampered by pain or stress – then it may sink into despair, and, eventually, death.

In Kim's case, however, the problems presented by suturing were of minor degree when compared with those concerned in the operation itself.

Despite my forced extensive acquaintance with the anatomy of animals over the whole range of species, I was astounded by the strength and thickness of the lioness's tissues, and the resistance they presented to the scalpel. But the biggest surprise of all was the size of the abdominal wall.

We were fortunate in having with us at the time a visiting American, Professor Barnett Levy. He was an expert in his field – which happened to be dental pathology – but had very kindly agreed to act as my temporary assistant. To Barnett Levy, the spectacle afforded by the animal's massive proportions must have been not only impressive but probably somewhat alarming. Being so much of a contrast to his usual type of patient Kim could well have daunted a less stout-hearted man, but my friend certainly did not allow this to interfere with his efficiency.

Much exploration was necessary before we came to the decisive stage of the laparotomy, when I managed to pull the horns of the uterus up through the surgical wound. Next, we exposed the ovaries, and examined them. And then – and only then – did we find that the fears that had inspired the exercise had been ill-founded. We could find

Tiger on the Table

nothing – nothing at all – except one dead foetus. Our efforts, so it seemed, had been superfluous.

*

Looking back, I now realise that the mood of disappointment and self-criticism that followed the operation was largely uncalled for. Using hindsight, it is easy to feel that it would have been better for us to have left Kim to sort out her problems on her own, rather than subject her to surgery; but the situation was by no means so clear-cut at the time. In fact, in view of the animal's obvious discomfort, and the hazards to which she might have been exposed by non-intervention, we had no option but to make sure of her condition, and for this a laparotomy was essential.

Again, although our action had been based on a faulty premise, it provided in the long term some highly benevolent by-products.

For years, we had been dissatisfied with the layout of the lions' dens. Built in Victorian times they offered no facilities for the sort of observation that was vital if we were to observe when these animals were likely to commence parturition, and we had argued in vain for the installation of closed circuit T.V. Today, although this boon is still denied us, there is an infra-red camera-hold installed in some of the den ceilings, a 'spy in the sky' that will not only rule out the need for operations such as that performed on Kim, but will also reveal whether or not a lioness is suckling her young, and thus establishing the maternal link that is essential for their survival. In suckling, as in copulating, the lioness likes her privacy, and the 'spy' enables us to see whether she is conforming to nature, or whether it will be necessary to take immediate action and remove the cub in order to save its life.

First Catch Your Tiger

Another advantage derived from Kim's operation was that it led to lionesses no longer being housed so close to the crowd, and thus disposed of many of the stresses that such proximity imposed upon their nervous systems. Last, but not least, was the effect the operation had on reassuring us as to Kim's general fitness for breeding.

Less than two years ago, four lively little lion cubs made their appearance on the Zoo scene, and won the hearts of countless people the world over. Celebrated in newspapers, magazines and scientific papers, they were the latest additions to a very healthy family – the family whose mother was Kim.

Our well-intentioned intervention had done no permanent harm!

9. An Elephant Never Forgets

Before the new elephant pavilion was constructed – to replace the original Victorian building which had become almost decrepit – the elephants were housed in the Middle Gardens, in temporary underground dens. The arrangement was not ideal – the dens were extremely cramped – but in an era of financial stringency there was no reasonable alternative.

The work entailed in the conversion had been relatively simple. Ramps had been built in the space once occupied by the shelter's steps and a water tank had been constructed as an elephant bath. The security aspect was good: being an island surrounded by a dyke the terrace was escape-proof. However the new habitat had one big disadvantage: a disadvantage that was to involve the animals in a series of minor crises, better avoided, and was eventually to lead to tragedy.

'Elephant Isle' was a great attraction to the public. They were able to see the animals being fed, and did not hesitate to supplement their diet. But the three elephants of the time – Diksie the big African and two Indians, Lakshmi and Rusty – became highly competitive in their efforts to get at the delicacies. They would jostle each other, and crowd to the edge of the island, and rarely – and inevitably – one would slip off, or be nudged off, and find itself in the dyke. For the keepers this meant continual worry about the safety

First Catch Your Tiger

of their charges: it also meant the likelihood of having to hoist them back. There was no specific lifting equipment such as a suitable mobile crane for this purpose, and we had to rely upon the animal being fit enough to walk out, by climbing steps improvised from bales of straw.

We appealed to the public to help by not tempting the animals, but generally speaking our appeal was made in vain. The hard core of the self-styled animal-lovers took no notice at all, they seemed incapable of appreciating the harm they might be doing. Eventually, to discourage Diksie and her companions from their balancing act, we lined the island's edge with a variety of deterrents including sharpened stones and, at the nearest point to the public, a row of spikes. Alas, though seemingly so sensible, our effort had an unfortunate sequel. The ever-greedy Diksie, lunging forward to catch a bun, toppled over on to the spikes, tearing her abdominal wall.

Called by the keeper, I was on the scene almost immediately. The injury, I was relieved to find, was not too serious and required only suturing under local analgesia. Operating on the underpart of an elephant is not the happiest of tasks. It is rather like repairing the roof of a railway arch while perched underneath it, and in expectation of its imminent collapse. But Diksie was an excellent patient, and gave me little trouble: surprisingly her adverse reaction only became manifest later, when it was time to remove the sutures. The occasion provided me with one of the most frightening experiences of my life.

When I went into Diksie's den, I found her extremely restive. She was in a very nervous condition, and irritable as well. She was again given a topical anaesthetic, but it appeared to have little result. The keeper's words of

An Elephant Never Forgets

reassurance seemed to be unheeded, and were met by a toss of the head that boded ill for the future.

As I prepared to remove the sutures I was aware that she was following my movements, her eyes surveying me with a really mean intensity. She kept shifting her massive feet and Gargantuan body apparently aimlessly, but moving gradually towards the back of the den. And then, quite suddenly, I realised that this nervous manoeuvring had a sinister purpose. Diksie was boxing me in.

An elephant, when aroused, can be a cunning foe. It can either lift you up with its trunk, and hurl you to the ground – to be trampled beneath its feet – or else it can resort to a more subtle method. Without your noticing the purposeful pattern of its footwork it will edge you toward a corner; and then, when it has positioned you, it will quietly sit down on top of you. Diksie, I realised with a pang of utter terror, was about to crush me to death!

Frantically, I glanced towards the door: only to find myself completely cut off from it, and from the keeper too. There was no getting at Diksie: the den fitted her like a glove. I could not climb over her: there were only two or three inches between her shoulders and the ceiling. I couldn't pass underneath her: she would use me as a cushion. And I could not walk around her, she formed a living barrier. As her massive grey bulk began to sag to administer the crushing coup de grace, I seized at the only option left to me, and bolted for the escape tunnel.

This was a narrow lane, formed by a brick wall built in parallel with the back wall of the den. It was roofed over, and connected Diksie's quarters with those of her next-door neighbour the Indian elephant Lakshmi. As I darted towards this refuge, my patient dropped all pretence at innocence and went berserk.

First Catch Your Tiger

She lunged at me with her tusks, and narrowly missed. Her keeper made one last effort to restrain her, only to be sent swaying with a blow from her flanks. A wise man, he made the only sensible reaction: in conformity with the instructions governing the behaviour of keepers when confronted by an animal out of control, he shot out of the door and bolted it behind him. I was now on my own.

I managed to reach the tunnel – I still don't know how – and, as I did so, the impact of Diksie's tusks on the brickwork created a tremor of shock that could be felt like a minor earthquake. Then came an angry scream from the cow-elephant, and the thud of her hind feet, stamped in rage. 'I'm safe,' I thought stupidly, 'I've got away with it.' Such optimism was quickly corrected. The commotion had excited Lakshmi. She, too, was frightened and angry. As she stamped around in her den, barring the exit, I realised the facts of my situation: I was caught between the two elephants like the meat inside a sandwich.

There are times when the knowledge of an opponent's behaviour pattern is not an unmixed blessing, and this was one of them. I knew what to expect of an hysterical and angry elephant, and the thought terrified me.

An elephant can be an unrelenting foe. Within seconds Diksie's trunk was searching along the tunnel like a tentacle, and I realised that the worst of my fears was justified. Unable to squeeze herself into the narrow escape-route she was aiming to drag me out of it. For the first time in my life I experienced the paralysis that comes from intense fear. I felt incapable of movement.

Both of the elephants were bellowing, and in the confined space of the den, the noise was horrifying. My hands and face were shamelessly running with sweat.

An elephant's trunk is an organ of extraordinary versa-

An Elephant Never Forgets

tility. It can lift tremendously heavy objects, and carry them for many miles, yet is so accurate, and so sensitive, that it can pick up a penny. This flexibility I had often admired and wondered at: but now the knowledge of what a questing trunk could do only added to my dreadful state of panic.

Those trunks came in from both entrances to the tunnel. Feverishly, as their rubbery hose-wide shapes came searching for me, I tried to cope with the rising sickness in my stomach, and recover from the weakness that had afflicted my limbs. To faint, I realised, would be absolutely fatal. The animals were missing me by only a few inches, so that the slightest tilt sideways would have put me inside their grasp. And once *that* happened, there would be no hope of survival: I would be plucked out of hiding, and brought to death on the den floor. But apart from this resolution – to keep conscious – I was incapable of any form of constructive thought. My adrenalin content was high, like that of a hunted animal . . .

I do not know how long I stayed in the tunnel, that escape-line that could so easily have become a fatal trap. Three minutes . . . ten . . . I have no idea at all. I was in a state of trance until, very dimly, I became conscious of men's voices, alternately shouting and coaxing, followed by a metallic echo, almost subconsciously identified as a den door slamming open.

Then, suddenly, Lakshmi's bellowing anger had diminished – or at least her trumpetings had become sensibly weaker – and somebody was calling my name and asking if I was all right.

It transpired that the keeper, having collected reinforcements, had returned to the scene, where he had very sensibly decided that the first thing to do was to get Lakshmi out of her den, and tethered to one of the rings outside the house.

First Catch Your Tiger

This achieved, I would be able to escape into the empty den.

'You all right, sir?'

'Yes,' I answered, though with considerable effort. 'Yes, I'm all right!'

A few seconds later I emerged from the tunnel, staggered limply through the den and came out, still shaking, into the open air, only half-believing in my narrow escape, and completely exhausted.

It took a while to get Diksie to quieten down. This normally lovable animal – a great favourite with the children – had temporarily turned killer. Incensed by my escape, she would not be lightly placated, and reacted by attacking the doors of her cell. It was an impressive performance, and a very grim reminder of what I'd missed. What with the clang of her tusks against the steel, her shrill screams of rage and complaint, and the stamping of her feet against the concrete of the floor, the 'orchestra' was loud enough to have been heard in Camden Town. And yet, when her passion eventually subsided, the change was almost unbelievably extreme.

Diksie's keeper led her gently up the ramp and brought her to a halt beside the tethering rings, where she allowed herself to be secured without the faintest sign of protest. And then, after I had steadied my hand, I took her sutures out.

In human surgery you can invite your patient to a preliminary discussion. You can tell him what you are going to do, and explain to him than an operation will be beneficial. There are no such palliatives for the animal patient's fear. Under its stress, and in the absence of any escape or release from it, he reverts immediately to savagery. Nor will he be mollified by the operation's success: he will identify you only as the maker of his pain. In surgery upon animals there is no such reward as a 'thank you'.

Aiding Diksie resulted in her having a continuing hatred of me. Although there was no repetition of her attempt to kill me, her hostility was implacable, and this, I felt, was a pity. Diksie was a very intelligent animal, and an artful one too. I enjoyed watching her techniques of evasion when confronted with situations that she wished to avoid, and particularly did I admire her expertise in detecting, and rejecting, medicines and drugs.

Not only do animals have a far more acute sense of taste and smell than that possessed by man – they have a far greater facility in detecting when their food or drink has been adulterated. But Diksie's sensitivity in this respect was really phenomenal, making mock of all our efforts to deceive her. On one occasion, after her keeper had tried repeatedly, and vainly, to administer a needed medicament by mixing it with her food, I devised what I thought was a perfect camouflage, impossible to detect. Diksie's 'likes' in food were extremely catholic. She was by no means faddy and would take anything she could get. But her particular weakness was for apples, and this I decided to play on.

Wearing rubber gloves so as to avoid contaminating them with scent, I slit open and pithed an apple with a scalpel blade, and inserted the medicine almost as deep as the core. This done, I pressed the ends of the slim gap together and sealed it with a rich layer of apple juice. The apple was then thrown into a bucket with more than two dozen others, all of the same variety, and so shuffled that not even I could spot the 'loaded' specimen.

The keeper duly started to feed the cunning Diksie, and she responded with apparent relish. One by one the apples disappeared until finally, to my delight, the bucket was empty: success, so it seemed, had been achieved at last. But just as I was about to deliver the keeper a little homily on the value of employing one's imagination, before withdrawing on a note of victory and modest understatement, Diksie once more confounded all our artifice. Slowly she opened her mouth, and delicately her trunk extracted from her cheek one carefully stored rosy apple, the one with the drug inside it. A thoughtful silence followed.

'You seen what I mean, sir,' the keeper eventually ventured. 'Our Diksie's a sight too clever for the likes of you and me . . .'

Diksie was a great favourite with children. Indeed she was a star attraction with all who came to visit the site, except on those occasions when her greed, or reaction to boredom, exceeded her good manners, and her instinctive sense of theatre involved the audience in her act.

Repeatedly we had asked the public to be careful about what they offered the elephants – some natural 'humorists' had even taken to giving them bottle-tops and other lethal titbits. And similarly we had warned the public not to get within the range of Diksie's trunk, which she employed to acquire practically anything that attracted her beady gaze. Umbrellas in particular brought out the worst in her, and served it would seem to titillate her palate. If Diksie saw an umbrella within her reach, she would hook the thing in seconds, and treat it as you or I would treat a stick of celery. You would hear the stick snap, as she tossed it into her mouth, and then, with apparent enjoyment, she would wreck it.

For her keepers this practice was the source of much embarrassment, entailing the maximum of apologetic 'explanations.' Sometimes, however, our sympathies were

An Elephant Never Forgets

entirely with the elephant: some visitors seemed dedicated to the pursuit of trouble. I myself have seen the most 'respectable' characters – 'respectable' in appearance I should add – behave like children, and cruel children at that, when confronted by the elephants. They would yell at them, attempt to goad them, even attempt to prod them in their trunks: and yet, when the animals exacted a reprisal, these were the very first to raise complaint. One day, when accosted by a particularly notorious representative of this lunatic fringe, and having listened to a tirade that lasted far too long, I thoroughly lost my temper. 'Damn your umbrella!' I exploded. 'I'm worried about our elephant!'

Few of the many spectators who gathered daily around Elephant Island to admire, feed and, sometimes, goad and taunt its inmates ever saw Diksie in one of her furies. Her occasional displays of primeval anger and savage ferocity were reserved for backstage, the privacy of her den. But some idea of the intensity of her passion, and the power that lay behind her imposing tusks, was given us when she quarrelled with the Indian elephant, Rusty. Diksie charged the door of Rusty's cell, and hit it so hard that she holed it. By the time her tantrums were over, the steel plate looked as though it had been torn apart by armour-piercing shells.

Diksie's end was a tragic one. It was not caused by her fighting moods: nor was her weakness for umbrellas responsible. It was an end that, perhaps, could have been prevented.

Despite the mishap that had led to her stomach injury, and the crazed outburst of anger that had followed it, Diksie's habit of over-reaching herself when on the island's shore remained as compulsive as ever, and repeatedly she and her companions had to be rescued from the dyke. Thus, when the new Elephant Pavilion was being built, I suggested that it be equipped with sky hooks. My suggestion proved to be incapable of execution. It was argued that considerable cost would be involved in strengthening the building's ceiling to take the hooks, and that such expense could not be justified: I also suggested we should have a suitable mobile crane, but this, I was told, would be providing for a contingency that might never happen. Unfortunately, this decision was challenged by events.

It was shortly after I had left the Zoo that the occasion we had feared, and warned against, eventually came to pass. Reaching out for a bun, Diksie overbalanced, and fell into the outside dyke.

This time she didn't get up.

According to newspaper reports twenty-eight men spent four hours of back-breaking labour in vain efforts to save the veteran elephant, a Zoo inmate since the day she'd arrived from Kenya, twenty-two years before. The light mobile crane mounted on a lorry that was the Zoo's sole lifting device was also employed, but its span was too narrow for the job, which resolved itself into a primitive tug of war.

After rigging a block and tackle, twenty-four of the men pulled frantically from the island against Diksie's three ton weight while four others went into the moat itself to fit her with a harness and endeavour to prop her up. But the exercise was fruitless, despite their devoted toil. Diksie was dead before they managed to lift her . . .

The post-mortem was thorough, and, it seems from reports, took many hours to complete. Diksie's right tusk had broken off, and she had suffered concussion when she hit the front wall of the moat. Her left leg had been badly broken, and a main nerve severed. And yet, despite this

An Elephant Never Forgets

comprehensive report of a series of serious injuries – each of them sufficient in itself to militate the chances of rescue – one may be forgiven for wondering if this tragic end to an animal that had achieved such a major place in the affections of the Zoo's public might still have been averted had more importance been given to the provision of suitable lifting apparatus. It will never be known how many of her injuries were caused by struggling in the dyke as apart from the fall.

It was not as though we were without practical experience of the difficulties involved in trying to lift really heavy animals by manual means alone. In fact the original suggestion for the installation of sky hooks had been based on the problems encountered in a previous rescue bid: one made to assist Rusty, an elephant suffering acutely from colic . . .

Called to Rusty's underground den in the old Elephant House, I realised immediately the difficulties of the job. The elephant had panicked when taken ill, and had fallen on its side. It had tried to get up, but couldn't – there wasn't sufficient room – and was now in a really pitiable condition.

Even in the most favourable circumstances it is an unacceptable risk for an elephant to be allowed to lie down for long. The huge quantities of grass that form its staple diet quickly ferment in the warmth of its stomach, and when the animal is in a prone position its processes of excretion cannot operate: they are restrained by its avoirdupois and by mounting gas pressure on the diaphragm. Six hours it is said is the maximum period it can sustain such a condition and live: unable even to break wind, its internal organs will distend and cause unbearable pressures on her heart and lungs.

On this occasion, however, our patient's plight was

aggravated by a move that the veterinary section had initiated – a move that, ironically, had been introduced as a means of improving the hygiene of the temporary dens and the health of the inmates.

We found the old den floors to be ill drained and badly surfaced. Their facilities for drainage were so inadequate that the elephants were suffering from a necrotic condition of the feet, caused by their having to stand in their own excrement.

To remedy this we had installed a floor of Derbyshire bluestone tiling. The criss-cross pattern joins between the tiles helped act as outlets and made the floors far easier to clean. But though the animals were quickly cured of their foot troubles as a result of this innovation, in the present instance its very virtues created physical torment for our patient. In its fright, the elephant was frantically turning round and round on its side, and each time it did so the razor-sharp tiles scraped and tore at its skin.

It was plain that our first priority must be to get the animal on its feet, and keep it there: but how could this be achieved? We ordered that the roof of the den be removed: we must try and lift the animal from the top.

For this purpose we rigged up a block and tackle, utilising for the purpose a number of hollow scaffolding tubes. Then, when the device was completed, I entered the den. My purpose was to fit a figure of eight harness around the elephant: a task that soon assumed the qualities of a nightmare.

No textbook includes advice on how to fix a figure of eight harness on an animal weighing three tons and more; an animal that, moreover, is suffering from a bowel complaint, is absolutely terrified, and is frenziedly thrashing around in a space so narrow and confined that it can't adopt

An Elephant Never Forgets

a standing posture on its own because it lacks the room. I had to learn the harness routine by a process of trial and error.

I had a cord attached to the end of the rope that ran from our home-made contraption, and fixed to the cord, was a long thin wire. With this firmly clutched in my hand, I found I had to lie on my belly, with my head pressed into the elephant's back in order to follow its cumbersome revolutions. And then, somehow, I must pass the cord, the rope, the wire, around the animal – conforming to the pattern of the eight – before fixing it to the hook that would (so we thought) pull our patient upright.

It was a complicated operation, carried out in a most unsatisfactory environment. The poor elephant was screaming all the time it was in progress but I dared not sedate her because it might then have been impossible to get her out. Meanwhile, the nature of her illness gave real offence to my nostrils, and irreparable damage to my clothes.

To get the hook inserted in the harness imposed a further stress on nerves and temper. To reach the hook I had to stand on the top of the elephant, a platform about as unstable as a ship in a storm. It was raining heavily, and vertically. I seemed to be balanced beneath a waterfall. By the time I was able to give the order to lift, I was so disenchanted that I had almost ceased to care. Even then, our problems were far from ended.

At first, things seemed to be going well with the actual lifting exercise. Steadily the animal was inched up until it reached an angle of forty-five degrees to the floor. And then there was a pause, and I heard an ominous creaking.

I had been assured that the lifting scaffolding would take up to five tons weight, a comfortable lifting margin of nearly half as much again as we required. This calculation now proved to be a wild overstatement. The creaking was followed by a resounding crash, and the whole of our apparatus fell dramatically apart. Once more the suffering elephant hit the floor, and almost hit me as it did so!

Our patient would die if it had to rely on our resources alone. When I joined my colleagues on the surface I found that we were all agreed on *that*. Help, outside help, was needed, and needed fast; but how to get it? Already we were perilously near the animal's deadline. Further delay would be fatal. Then one of us suggested that we try the 600 Group, and I got on to the telephone. Could they lend us, please, one of their commercial cranes? When we told them what it was for, their response was generous, and prompt.

A huge thing – a real mechanical monster – the very appearance of the crane gave us all an injection of confidence. With such an awesome aid, we could have tackled elephants by the herd. Its jib was so long that it reached right across from the Outer Circle. It passed right over the power-lines, to hover over the roofless den. Once more I ventured to the patient's side.

This time there were no hitches. The driver could not see his objective, but got the crane into position by following hand signals from one of our staff, putting him 'on target.' The lift itself was flawless, and soon the elephant was on her feet. To make sure that she did not fall again, we wedged her in her upright posture by filling the den with straw bales. To doubly ensure against accident, we also placed a cross beam over the opening in the roof, and 'anchored' her to it by a rope.

When the job was nearly finished I encountered one of the overseers, and said to him conversationally, 'Mr Vinall, it is raining very hard!'

He answered simply, 'With respect, sir, it is pissing down!'

Kumari, the tigress, and her cub Suki.

Kumari on the table, after initial anaesthesia.

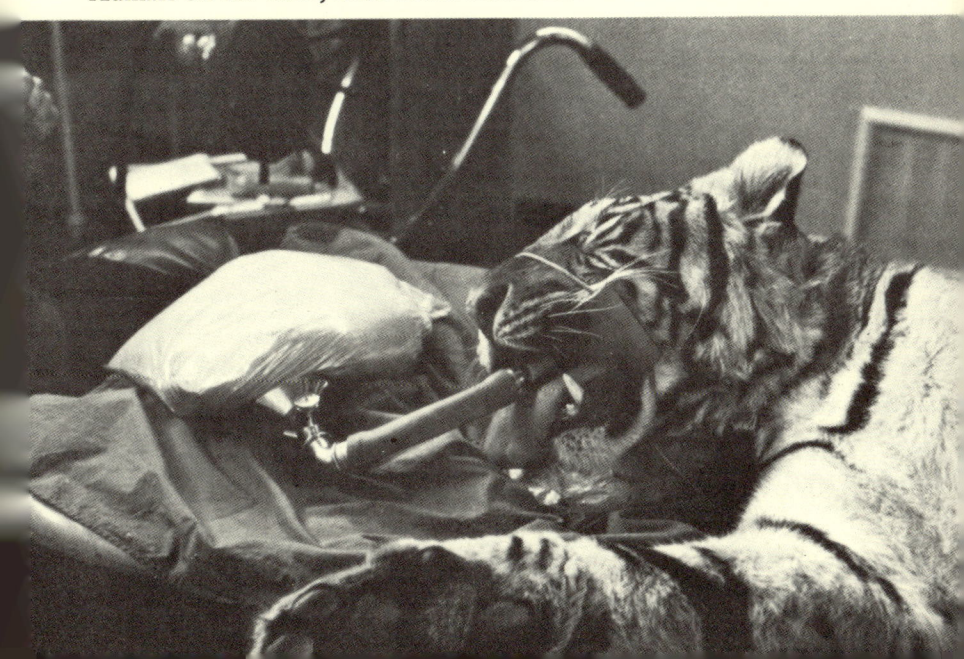

Kim, the lioness, with Mark at the Zoo.

Diksie: the problem.

The disaster: an attempt is made to raise Diksie to her feet.

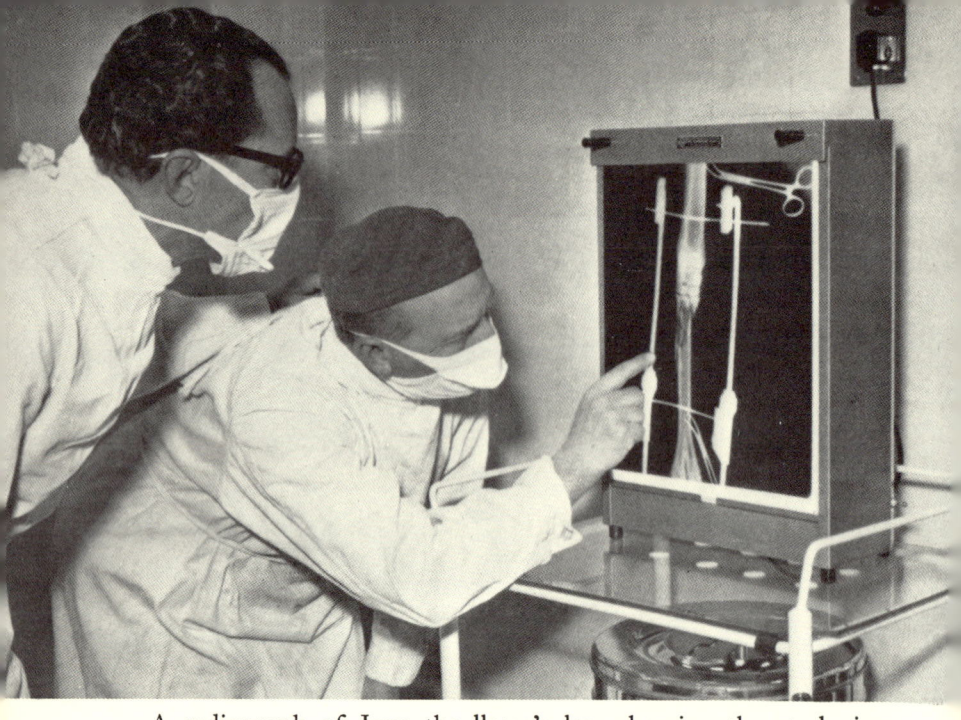

A radiograph of June the llama's leg, showing the steel pins mounted through the bones on to a surgical extension apparatus.

The pins are removed several weeks after the operation.

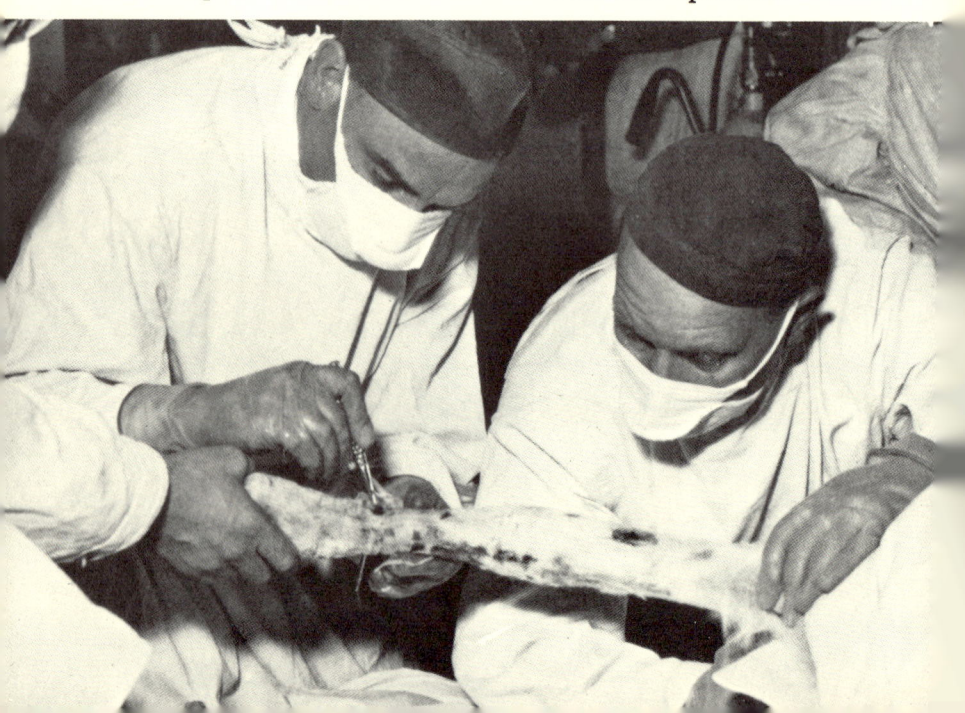

An Elephant Never Forgets

It struck me that an even stronger verb was required to describe the physical reaction of our patient.

Insurance agents show little enthusiasm for exploring the veterinary profession in their search for clients. In some companies the risk rating is as high as that placed on a steeplejack. Considering the chances of accident to the veterinary man, their attitude is fairly understandable. On paper at least, he is vulnerable to a multitude of hazards – from the kick of a restless carthorse to an infectious disease, e.g. brucellosis. However, in applying surgery to wild animals, the dangers of accident to the surgeon – not to mention his staff! – are largely related to the speed with which some animals regain consciousness from anaesthetics.

We know a considerable amount about the behaviour of domestic animals, such as dogs and cats, and we are aware of the correct anaesthetic to give them. We also know much about their speed of recovery, and their likely attitudes when emerging from sedation. But wild animals have a far higher viability than that of the household pets, and their reactions and capacities vary considerably – not only between species and species, but between animals of the same stock. Even now we are only on the fringe of understanding the complex motivations of the untamed. Neither the textbook, nor personal experience, can provide us with an all-embracing rule of treatment, suitable for universal application. One learns as one goes.

One of the most significant examples I encountered of the way in which one can become complacent regarding one's capacity for judging the right degree of anaesthesia arose when I was examining a tigress.

10. Creatures Great and Small . . .

The encounter with the tigress followed a report from her keeper, who had noticed she had developed a limp. He could see no reason for this – the animal bore no surface trace of injury – and our own preliminary investigation was equally unrewarding. We therefore decided to hospitalise and anaesthetise her and conduct a careful examination.

After sedating her, and administering an intravenous anaesthetic we found a tiny penetration wound on the left carpal joint. We had the paw radiographed, and a lesion on the distal extremity of the radius was revealed. We then decided to aspirate the joint's fluid, in order to ascertain the nature of any infection that might exist.

The operation was quite a simple one, and after the patient had been injected with further pentathol, the carpal area was incised, the paw held while, with a needle and syringe, we commenced to draw away the fluid. Then, suddenly, I found our positions had been reversed. The tigress was becoming conscious, and was now holding *my* hand, and not exactly affectionately at that!

Happily for the future of my career, I managed to disengage: but the incident was upsetting. After eight years of experience of the complexities involved in the anaesthetising of wild animals, I had fallen victim to the over-confidence against which I had so often warned others. The lesson was one I resolved not to forget.

From that time onwards, I introduced the most stringent measures of ascertaining the appropriate dosage for each individual patient, and recorded diligently the details of their daily behaviour pattern. For the carefully programmed and highly-skilled observation that alone could make those measures meaningful, I relied, as I did for so many other aspects of sick care, on the staff of the hospital and the individual keepers. Yet, even so, there was the occasional faulty estimate: and to such mis-readings the perverse activities of the more intelligent species greatly contributed. Distrustful of our well-meant activities, the great apes in particular did their best to confuse the calculations on which we based their treatment. They would detect, and refuse, drugs offered for oral transmission. Or else they would pretend to be soporific when they definitely were not. There seemed to be no end to their capacity for mischief.

A drug that can be tasteless, and colourless too . . . a drug that dissolves easily, and is immediate in its action . . . we have all of us seen this sort of wonder-product in the television thrillers. In real life it does not exist. This conclusion follows much patient – and initially hopeful – searching for such a panacea: each time there has been disillusionment as sequel.

What appeared to be the most promising development towards our ideal objective came to us in the 'sixties, when a continental firm claimed to have produced a sedative that was not only undetectable by taste and smell but capable of rendering its recipient unconscious 'within less that ten minutes.' Although we received this statement with initial scepticism, being accustomed by then to disappointment, the company's confidence tended to be eventually infectious. The firm was of good repute, we all knew its chemists were responsible men of integrity. Moreover, the

First Catch Your Tiger

high price placed on the product was in itself a cause of 'impressment': at £2.10.0d. per ampoule it *must* be better than most! So at last we decided to give the sedative a trial, and chose for patient and 'guinea-pig' the most suspiciously inclined of all our guests, a sub-adult male gorilla.

The usual range of barbiturates and bromides would not have fooled this extremely wary character. The bitterness of the barbiturate, and the extremely unpleasant flavour of the bromide, would have caused him to reject such offerings with contempt. There was no camouflaging them from his discerning tongue and nose. Yet, when we tried the new drug, our unhandleable gorilla raised not a single protest. He drained the orange juice that contained the dosage in one single blissful gulp. We were most impressed.

Next, however, came the need for the drug to prove itself fast-acting, and the 'ten minutes' promise of its makers appeared to be more than a little over-optimistic. After twenty minutes there was still no reaction from the animal. After forty, we had become resigned to failure. And then, without warning, our patient flopped on to the floor.

In all cases involving critical anaesthesia we followed a safety routine in which it was my rule that I always 'went in first' – entering the den to decide whether it would be safe for the others to follow. As the one best qualified to assess the state of the animal, I had insisted on this as an essential in a programme that, though at times it may have seemed to be a little over-cautious was on this occasion to prove itself as based on well-founded fears. Sometimes I wore a safety rope around my waist with appropriate instructions to pull me out if necessary. This time, it didn't seem necessary.

When I entered the den, it seemed that the drug had been one hundred per cent effective. When I turned the gorilla on

Creatures Great and Small...

to his back he showed no resistance: he was breathing evenly, and heavily, and was seemingly deeply narcotised.

I went through the rest of the procedure, and checked on his eyes and his reflexes: these too appeared to confirm my opinion, that sedation was complete. I then signalled my assistants that the time had come to move him.

They brought him to the operating theatre, propping him up between them by the arms. Briefly they paused in the doorway as I went towards the operating theatre, and then, in a second, all hell broke loose!

The beast jerked himself upright, seemingly, for the moment, fully conscious and full of fight! I had a brief impression of his fur-matted chest – apparently swelling to twice its normal size – and his eyes, standing out as if at the end of cornstalks, and then, throwing his arms wide, he dashed his 'guards' to the floor. Glaring madly, and with mouth wide open, he came through the doorway, and charged straight at me – like a train from out of a tunnel!

My self-control vanished, and I grabbed wildly for a 'weapon.' My hands closed on the handle of a broom. Desperately I thrust it before me, as the gorilla loomed up, and was promptly sent reeling back against the wall. The animal had attacked with such force that he had stumbled on to the broomhead, and driven it into his stomach.

There was a full-throated bellow of fury, as he cannoned off the broom into his recently vacated den, and then – with complete unexpectedness – he fell flat on his face and lay still.

My colleagues got up, looking extremely shaky. I felt very shaky myself, and very puzzled too. For a gorilla to have knocked himself out with a broom was a truly extraordinary feat, but was, I felt, a little too good to be true. Sure enough, on inspection it transpired that it was the drug, not the broom, that had felled him, and transformed him so dramatically into a horizontal gorilla.

The gorilla's emergence from sedation had been of very short duration, but had lasted long enough to give us all a bad fright, and had served to emphasise yet again the necessity of all-round reliability in the type of narcotic employed for an animal not far removed from the wild. The criteria of a suitable sedative is that it must be consistent in its performance: it must 'work' every time it is used, and be consistent throughout its use. It must possess regularity of action, with no variation. And it must carry a wide safety margin. The continental drug failed to measure up to such requirements. It was, we decided, of limited use to the Zoo.

Unlike the civilised and sophisticated human, an animal seldom fails to give warning of hostile intent. It may be conveyed by the way he looks at you, the swish of his tail, the manner of his walk, or a score of other ways, depending on the species: but the warning is there, if only you can recognise it. However, even the most skilled observers may sometimes fail to recognise the threat until it is too late to ward against it, while at other times the confrontation is created by sheer chance.

One of the oddest instances of how suddenly a situation in the operating theatre can change from routine to menace occurred when we were operating on a lioness.

We had administered a gas anaesthetic, maintained via an endotracheal tube, and although inserting the tube into the animal's open mouth – from which it travels down into the trachea – may be considered a little daunting, for us it was a fairly commonplace procedure. We certainly did not anticipate it would be accompanied by drama, but this was to be the exception to the rule.

Creatures Great and Small . . .

The administration went off smoothly at the beginning, and would doubtless have continued to do so if something had not arisen that was completely unexpected. The unconscious animal suddenly suffered a respiratory spasm. There came a tremendous sneeze – and the tube blew out!

The situation escalated with amazing speed. Almost immediately the lioness, receiving no anaesthetic gases, opened a bleary eye. A second later she began to move her limbs. As she raised herself on the table the theatre echoed to a mighty roar.

Somehow we recovered our scattered thinking processes. Taken so shamefully by surprise, we had now to react with sharpness. An emergency mask, always available, was positioned over the angry face, and the anaesthetic gases turned on. Soon the patient was restored to harmless slumber and intubated again.

What with tigers attempting to hold him by the hand, gorillas anxious to squeeze the life out of him, and lionesses sitting up on the operating table, the veterinary surgeon's lot may sometimes seem unenviable. Both he and the members of his theatre team must be ready at all times for defensive action – against dangers unencountered when practising upon man. They must be prepared to meet contingencies that turn critical in seconds, converting the patient into a savage foe. All the same, there have been occasions when this stress on conflict may seem to be overdone, and the surgeon's acquired wariness made into a bit of a joke. One such was when Prince Philip visited the hospital – to be confronted by a weapon reminiscent of gang warfare . . .

Escorted to the operating theatre, Prince Philip crossed over to the table, to glance with apparent interest at my array of surgical implements, neatly arranged in a glass

First Catch Your Tiger

cupboard beside it. And then he gave an unexpected laugh.

Puzzled, I followed the direction of his gaze, and saw that in the midst of the instruments had been placed an ugly knuckleduster!

I had brought the thing home from Italy, as a souvenir of the war, and illegally had kept it for years in the drawer of my desk. Now certain humorists on my staff had stealthily abstracted it, and put it on display for the royal occasion.

'Well,' said the Prince, 'I suppose it's your idea of an anaesthetic. But I have never before seen a knuckleduster in a cupboard for surgical instruments.'

*

What sort of case gave me the greatest satisfaction? I was once asked this question by a visiting V.I.P. who promptly followed up with a series of supplementaries. Was I more pleased with a success on a really handsome animal – a lion, say, or a tiger? Or did I prefer to deal with one of the uglier species? But perhaps I found it more interesting to operate on birds? Or did the repulsive reptiles make any sort of appeal?

This earnest interrogation, conducted at some pace, deserved, I felt, a well-considered answer. Of course every surgeon has his preferred type of operation, usually the one presenting the greatest challenge to his skill, but never before had I considered that I might also have 'preferences' for certain types of patient. However, I eventually replied that, just as the size of an animal is not necessarily related to the size of the problem it poses, neither is one's professional satisfaction in helping it influenced by its looks, good or otherwise.

Put like that, my argument may have sounded a little pompous. It was also, I now realise, only partly true.

Creatures Great and Small...

Professionally, it is as satisfying for a surgeon to remove an abdominal tumour from a budgerigar, as I have done, using a hair-grip for a surgical clip, as it is for a watchmaker to operate on a watch while it is still ticking. Each in its own way is the epitome of transistorised surgical skill. To carry out a colostomy on a snake is to me a more difficult process, and therefore more rewarding than, say, repairing the fractured leg of a tiger. But this does not mean that I prefer the snake's appearance to that of the handsome tiger: the question of preferences does not come into the matter. A surgeon's satisfaction is – and must be – related to the nature of the challenge, and his degree of success in meeting it. Seldom, if ever, is it derived from his having healed an animal that he 'likes' better than another.

But, this said, I would emphasise that this philosophy – for want of a better word – applies solely to operations on wild animals. One's feelings become more inhibited – one becomes aware of a personal involvement – when the patient is domesticated, a household pet.

The household pet, however humble, is of importance not only to itself but also to the person who owns it. It is part of the family circle, a symbol of family affection, and as such its health and well-being affects the happiness of all members of that family. But the wild animal, whatever the sentimentalists may say, matters in the ultimate to itself alone. For the surgeon there is only the minimum of personal association.

Nobody 'owns' the captive wild animal, except in the strictly legal sense of the word. A zoo has a responsibility for it, as something on its 'books': a stamp in its collection that may be precious or rare. The veterinary surgeon has a responsibility towards it; that which the strong must always have for the weak. But its keeper alone has the type of responsibility that can grow into affection – an affection stemming from the fact that he is in daily contact with it, and watchful of all its moods. He looks on it protectively and it assumes, in his eyes, a domesticated status: it is associated with him as one of his group. In all other respects, however, the zoo animal is an orphan, with no status of its own, and the surgeon has only the briefest acquaintance with it, at the time when its greatest fears are preying on it. To the surgeon, there is then neither time, need nor room for sentiment: his only feelings are of the immediacy and urgency of the task in hand. To him, the patient is just one of many such: 6,000 animals collected by the Zoo a gathering of 'all creatures great and small'.

*

'All creatures great and small . . .' Glancing at one of my veterinary reports, taken at random, I find that in one quarterly period in 1962, no fewer than 33 cases were admitted to the Zoo's hospital while 29 patients were treated in their houses.

They ranged from a White Rhino which had lost its balance, and was found to be suffering from enterotoxaemia, to a White Pelican, shot in mid-flight, whose wing we were forced to amputate. They included a chinchilla, whose fractured femur was repaired by intramedullary fixation, using a hypodermic needle cut exactly to the length of the femur as revealed by X-ray. They also included an orang-utan with rickets, treated in collaboration with a famous London children's hospital.

A gentle tiger, who bruised his face against the bars in trying to show affection for his keeper . . . a spider monkey who was discovered to have T.B. . . . from a short-toed eagle with bumblefoot, to a spot-nosed monkey that had

Creatures Great and Small . . .

broken its tail, the 'creatures' came in all sizes, and kept us fully occupied.

One of the earliest patients of the new Zoo Hospital was also one of the most popular – June, the gentle-eyed and silky-haired eighteen year old llama, who spent most of her time towing children around the Gardens in a little cart.

Just after Christmas 1956, and during the night, this most amiable of animals somehow slipped sideways and caught her foot in the chainlink netting of the fence. Evidently she struggled hard to free herself, and when her keeper found her in the morning she was in very poor shape indeed. The lower part of her leg was dangling by its skin, and when we came to examine her, we discovered that the bones were so badly broken that it was like touching a bag of pebbles. June had broken her leg in twelve separate places, immediately below, and involving, the carpal joint. We decided on an orthopaedic operation.

Not many years before, all hope for June would have had to have been ruled out. Without the aid of sophisticated methods of anaesthesia, she would have had no chance of a recovery. Her fear and pain reflexes would probably have been sufficient in themselves ultimately to kill her, and our only decision would have been on a humane way of shortening the process. Even then, it was felt in one quarter that the kindest thing for our patient was to destroy her; but this we were unwilling to do. We felt certain that she still had a chance of life.

The procedure that was eventually adopted was a complex one mechanically, and, as in so many of the other things we did, we had no precedent to guide us.

It involved drilling holes transversally through the bone above the knee (the radius) and the large bone below the knee (the metacarpus). Through these holes was then inserted a stainless steel rod, sized to project just an inch on either side of the leg, above and below the knee. To these rods were attached the sideplates of a surgical orthopaedic 'rack'.

Then, by slowly applying the screw, the bars were gradually forced apart, with the effect that the leg was progressively tensed, finally becoming rigid.

Ultimately, by using the bars as a framework, we managed to get June's leg put into plaster.

The operation complete, we waited anxiously for the llama's reactions. Would she worsen her injuries by reacting violently against their alien covering? Would she panic – as animals do – at her temporarily altered balance? We need not have worried. June made a model patient, a really marvellous example of good-tempered fortitude. After two months we performed a second operation, removing the pins and plaster. . . .

Another unusual problem to confront us in those early days of the hospital was that posed by a female seal.

Attacked by the male during sexual display, she had decidedly got the worst of the encounter. When she was brought into hospital, she was in a serious state, with injuries to her head, face and flippers. We managed to patch her up without undue difficulty, but then had to solve a rather peculiar dilemma: namely how could we dress her injuries? A seal, to remain healthy, has to spend most of his time in the water. But this would make impracticable the dressings that we usually employed. They would be washed away as soon as our patient took a bath!

Eventually, our team came up with an answer. They suggested a specially treated powder, which was rapidly absorbed into the flesh. This would penetrate the injured areas before it could be washed off. We applied the powder,

Creatures Great and Small . . .

and were well-satisfied with the speed of its 'disappearance'. Then, as an extra precaution, we barred the seal from the pool, but kept her happy by frequently dousing her down with a hose. She was soon in good condition again.

One memorable out-patient was a baby gorilla, purchased for an extensive private zoo down in Kent. The animal had a pronounced swelling over the umbilicus, and the attending veterinary surgeon referred him to us for diagnosis and surgery. By doing so he was to make a unique contribution to the hospital's experience of difficult cases.

On examining the patient, we found him to be suffering from an umbilical hernia, and we arranged to operate on him to repair the defect.

There was absolutely no literature available on the rupture as related to apes, and we were delighted when a surgeon from a children's hospital came along to assist us. It was also arranged to film the whole process in colour. We envisaged considerable problems – and solutions – arising from so novel a sortie: in the event, however, we got even more than we had bargained for.

First among the many surprises we experienced was the gorilla's extraordinary lack of response to our attempts to sedate him. One hour after the first intramuscular injection he showed only moderate sedation. Our patient was still responsive to manipulation half an hour after the operation itself had been scheduled to begin.

Originally, we had hoped to follow up the sedation with light anaesthesia, using an intravenous injection, but the gorilla resented this, and began to struggle. We found it almost impossible to restrain him.

All this was disappointing, and in a sense anti-climactic. However, as a dubious expedient, we finally decided to try the effect of applying a face mask of the type employed on

First Catch Your Tiger

man. To our relief, the switch achieved its purpose, though not until the theatre had been treated to the somewhat ludicrous spectacle of our administering halothane and oxygen to the gorilla while it lay with its head reposing in the Hospital Superintendent's arms.

Once our patient was secured to the operating table we began our work in earnest: but here too we experienced disappointment. We had planned to insert an endotracheal tube into the gorilla's windpipe, but even the smallest type we had available was found to be too large. Our final resort was to use an open mask: its gauze being saturated by ethyl chloride.

However, despite such frustrations – perhaps inevitable in a process that was largely experimental – the operation itself turned out to be highly successful, and the gorilla, after being treated with antibiotic injections twice a day, made a splendid recovery. Pitting our wits against his, and to distract his attention from his operation wound, we strapped a hateful sticky bandage around his ankle. He was so 'intelligent' that he spent two days removing it, completely ignoring his stitches, thus allowing his surgical wound to heal undisturbed. Considerable interest in the affair was shown by a scientific journal and, as a result, the daily press made so much of it that it became a source of embarrassment. But certainly the operation was unique, and the lessons we had learned were duly recorded for those who might be called on to take similar action in the future.

Short-wave therapy to a camel . . . treatment of a tiger for muscular dystrophy . . . electric shock therapy for a lion . . . thanks to the co-operation of scientists, chemists, and leading exponents of human medicine and surgery, the Zoo Hospital was able to cater for the needs of specimens that ranged from the £14,000 panda to a minnow worth less

Creatures Great and Small . . .

than a shilling. Nor were its activities restricted to the Zoo's animals alone.

From homes and private zoos all over the country we had animals, birds and reptiles – wild beasts and household pets – referred to our busy out-patients' department. And for some of our most challenging cases we went to other zoos, including the Society's country zoo at Whipsnade. It was there that we were posed the problem of sedating a pregnant hippopotamus. . . .

11. Unhappy Hippos

Fifi, the temperamental young hippo, and Neville her middle-aged mate, whom she very much dominated, were former residents of Regent's Park who had been moved to Whipsnade because of our rebuilding plans. But the nervous and aggressive trends in Fifi's nature soon became manifest and it was not long before she was providing the Whipsnade authorities with a major headache.

The hippos' new keeper, Mr Stanbridge, was a man of great experience, and great competence, in the handling of hippopotami, but Fifi seemed to develop a perverse resentment of him, and translated this into action on every occasion that offered. She charged him when he arrived in the enclosure with her food. She charged him again when he attempted to coax and soothe her. Repeatedly she hurled herself at him in her violence, even attacking the steel bars that divided her swimming and feeding quarters in her frantic efforts to get at him.

Stanbridge bore without rancour these outrageous attacks. In the course of his long record of service to wild animals in captivity he had developed a tolerant and perceptive philosophy as regards the moods and caprices of his charges, and had observed that when the female of the species became temperamental, and showed aggression towards its keepers, it was usually when under the influence of considerable fear and stress. Fifi, he deduced correctly, was pregnant.

Fifi and her new mate at Whipsnade.

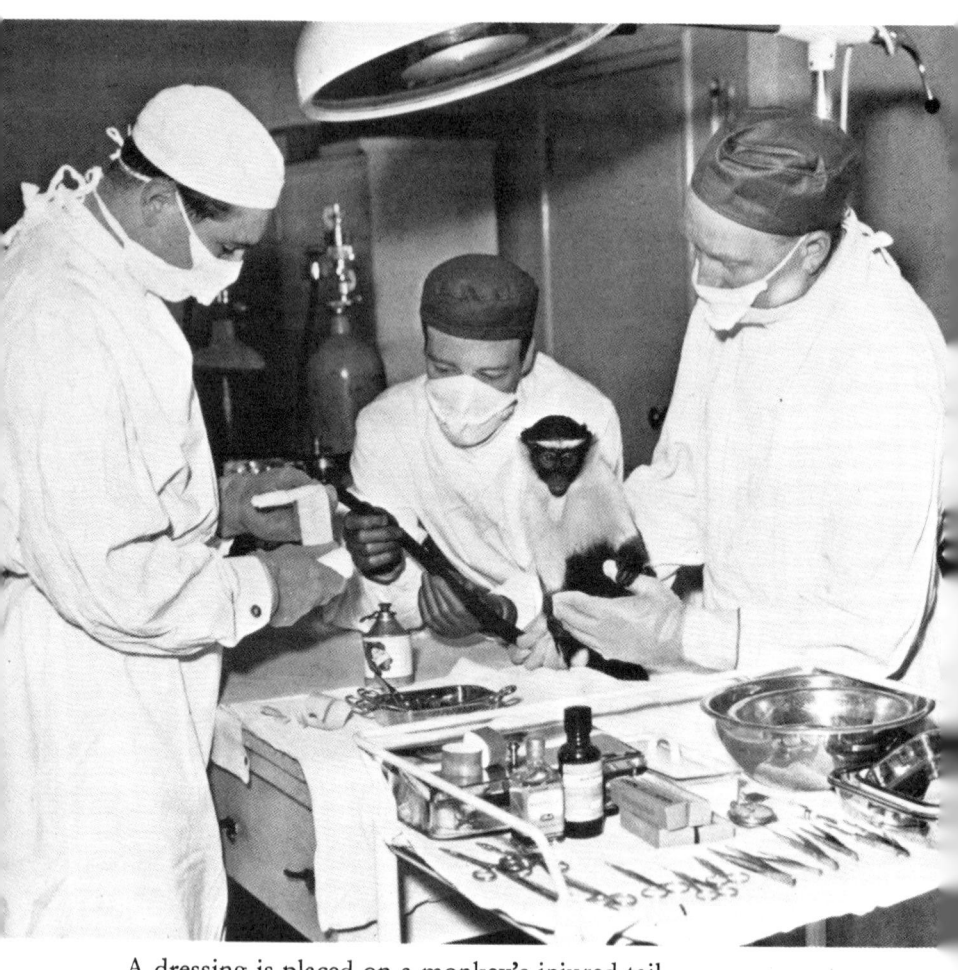

A dressing is placed on a monkey's injured tail.

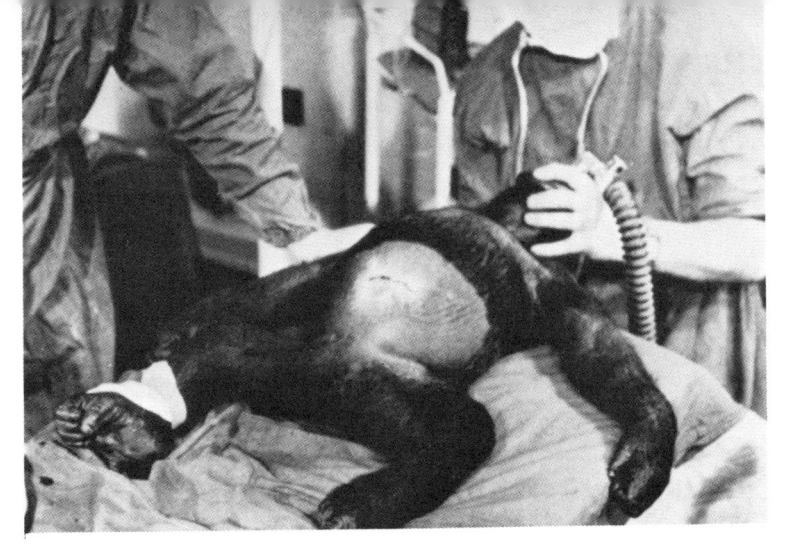

A baby gorilla after a hernia operation. The adhesive bandage on his right ankle kept him occupied trying to remove it for two days after the operation so that he left his operational wound alone.

A baby mountain gorilla in his cage at the Zoo.

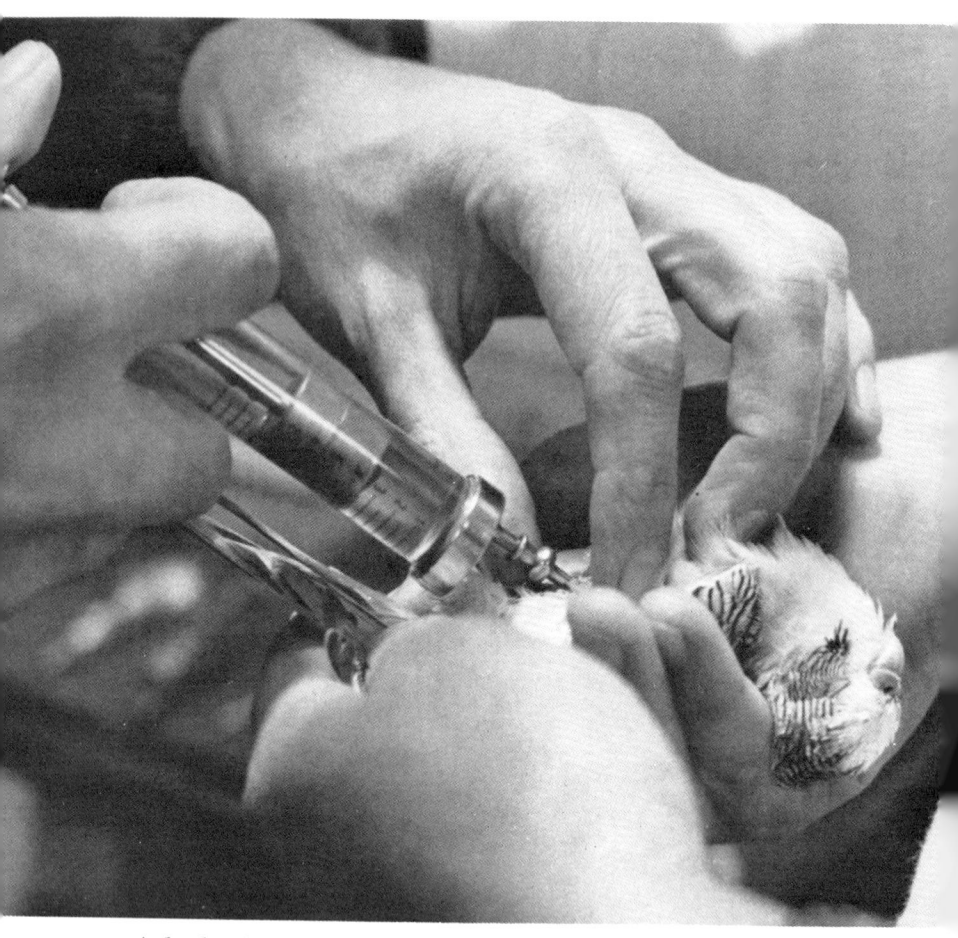

A budgerigar receives an intraperitoneal injection of an anaesthetic.

Unhappy Hippos

A little later, relaxation of the hippo's perivulvar tissue was observed and it was feared that in her violent moods she might injure herself and the foetus. As parturition drew near these fears increased. Fifi's fits of aggression became more and more frequent, and in accordance with the usual procedure at zoos when animals turn violent, it was decided to separate her from her mate. Neville's departure, however, failed completely to placate her. Instead of quietening down, she became so distressed that she almost wrecked the enclosure.

Anxious to allay this hysteria, which posed such a grave threat to her safety, the Zoo authorities then reversed their decision and re-united the pair, but here too they had failed to allow for the unpredictability of Fifi's nature. No sooner did her old mate return than she savagely attacked him, inflicting severe skeletal injuries.

Immediately after this, we conferred with the Whipsnade authorities. We found ourselves faced with a very real problem, involving a series of dilemmas, unusually complex.

To ascertain the nature of Neville's injuries, and do what we could to treat them, we would have to float him. We could do this easily enough, by filling the swimming tank, but such a move was likely to endanger the calf: a low water-level was essential for its safety after delivery.

Confronted by this prospect, and considering the apparent odds against the male's survival – treatment or no – it was suggested by one Zoo official that it would be better to shorten Neville's misery. Why not shoot him?

At this stage we disagreed. Quite apart from our instinctive desire to do something constructive for the damaged Neville, there was the prosaic consideration that the sound of the shot, and the noise occasioned by the need to remove

First Catch Your Tiger

his body from the water, would probably serve to further distress Fifi, and cause her to renew her murderous violence. Some other solution was needed.

Our objectives, we decided, could be broadly defined as follows: Firstly, we must save mother and calf from the consequences of the former's aggressive manifestations. Next, we should examine Neville's wounds, and, if at all possible, repair them. For success in either of these projects a prerequisite must be the effective sedating of Fifi.

But to sedate a hippo – a pregnant, nervous and thoroughly truculent hippo – presented difficulties as acute as those they were meant to surmount.

Ideally, the drug should be non-toxic to the mother and the foetus. It should not be cumulative as regards its effects, nor should it produce drug resistance. It was essential that the calmness it induced should not be such as to prevent the lively normal functioning of the patient's reflexes.

The administration of the drug presented similar complications, aggravated by the state of Fifi's temper. In most other cases we would have been able to carry out the close injection technique: but only a man who had tired of living would have dared approach our hippo in her current mood.

A projectile syringe – fired from a gun – would normally have been employed in conditions where a large animal had turned violent: but Fifi's pregnancy precluded this resort. The noise would upset the patient even more than she was upset already, and cause further hazard to the life of her calf. The drug, we agreed, must be administered orally, and this in turn created further problems.

To insure against its detection, it was necessary that the drug should not be unpleasant to the taste. Neither should it be strong-smelling. Fifi would be bound to reject anything that tasted, or smelled, in any way unusual. Furthermore it was essential that while the drug performed its function of allaying the patient's fear and apprehension, it did not do so at the cost of interfering with the psychological and physical requirements of parturition, or its mechanical procedures. Such stipulations – and qualifications – left us with a very limited choice.

The barbiturates we had to reject almost as soon as their use was suggested. Their hypnotic and sedative effect might well have been beneficial, but barbiturates are bitter to the palate. More, they can cross the placental barrier, to the detriment of the foetus.

Bromides, we decided, would be equally unacceptable. Not only are they evil-tasting: large doses of them would be required to induce pronounced sedation. We also ruled against the use of chloral hydrate, as being likely to create foetal anaesthesia. This left only the products of the tranquilliser group.

Commonly called ataractics, because they produce 'freedom from disturbance of the mind', it was known that some of them did not pass the placental barrier, and after reviewing the products of the phenothazine group we decided to take a chance on promazine hydrochloride. But how to estimate the correct dosage for a hippo? Needless to say the textbooks failed to come out with any answer.

However, in the hospital at Regent's Park, investigations had been carried out into dosage rates for animals in general, using drugs on a wide range of species, and the result of these investigations had indicated a possible minimum dose requirement of from four to five milligrammes per kilo body weight. In the absence of any more specific guidance we decided to use this general estimate as a norm for our hippo.

Fifi was a remarkably solid character, in the sense of physical bulk. Even by the generous standards prevailing among the hippopotami, she was buxom, to say the least. We had no record of her true weight, but estimated that she was heavier than her consort, who topped the scales at three tons.

Using this as a means of comparison, we then calculated that our patient would require a daily dose of 10 grammes and over – a truly tremendous dosage, fifty times the maximum that would be prescribed for a human.

This dramatic equation agreed, we went ahead with the 'treatment', mixing the drug in powdered form in Fifi's evening meal.

'Sedated' or no, the hippo, we felt, would be ready for yet another ferocious tantrum when we came to remove her mate from his watery bed. With the results of her former furies imprinted not only on our memories but also on the bars and walls of her ravaged enclosure, there was considerable apprehension of her capacity for further destruction. Yet, owing to her condition, we had to be wary of over-sedating; a move that could have had fatal consequences for her calf.

However, when the time came for us to enter the pool in order to make a preliminary inspection of the wounded male, Fifi accepted the situation and behaved quite calmly. Inevitably the team created – for all their efforts to the contrary – a certain amount of noise, but we need not have worried about its effect on our patient. Sedation was satisfactory.

To Neville, alas, no drug could bring assistance, and no amount of surgery could repair his fractured legs. The battered hippo was past all hope of aid, and had died before that aid could reach him. We retrieved his body, but Fifi

Unhappy Hippos

took no notice of our task: even that failed to arouse her from her drug-induced docility.

The birth of the calf, to whose future such thoughts had been given, was similarly unaccompanied by dramatics from its mother. It was, in fact, completely uneventful, and mother and daughter 'settled-in' quite comfortably.

A few days later, Keeper Stanbridge, whose skilled observations on the effects of the regime were quite invaluable, reported that Fifi was showing fresh signs of aggression: but this he put down to the maternal instinct, with our patient being anxious to protect her baby. Another cause for worry arose when it was observed that, after three or four weeks, the calf was nibbling at the drugged food left by its mother. Was there danger for the young one in this process? Happily Fifi's greed was so pronounced that the amount she left over from her meals was very small. On consideration we decided to continue as before.

When at last we released the hippos from their quarters and let them go into the outside paddock, we all felt a certain apprehension. But Fifi and her daughter entered the water quietly, jostling each other as if in sport. We breathed again . . .

The sort of trailer they used to employ for the old-time movies would probably have described the story of Fifi and Neville as one in which triumph and tragedy went hand in hand. Fifi's was the triumph: the tragedy was for Neville. When he had first come to the Zoo, in 1951, he settled in as the mate of Daisy, a hippo very well known to Zoo visitors, the thoughtlessness of one of whom eventually killed her.

A rubber ball was thrown to her – a titbit which she obligingly swallowed. Later this gave rise to a severe internal complaint, from which she died. How we all wish

First Catch Your Tiger

we could have forced the humorist responsible to have witnessed the grim results of his playful gesture.

Over the years, much time and effort was expounded by the hospital staff in trying to alleviate the effects on our animals of the misbehaviour of some of the visitors. Often the latter's actions were motivated by sheer ignorance, but sometimes deliberate cruelty was the cause.

One of the nastiest examples of the damage that can be inflicted by humans on captive animals occurred during a so-called 'record-breaking' bank holiday weekend when over 91,000 people visited the Zoological Gardens. Most of the holidaymakers came in pursuit of harmless entertainment, and some of them came for education too, but the rest could be split into two groups of undesirables, the sentimentalists (so-called) and the savages.

The former characters – contributing to a massive display of unsolicited benevolence that unloaded on the animals an estimated amount of over twelve tons of food – bestowed their bounty without any apparent thought as to its consequences, or its suitability, or otherwise, for its recipients.

Not unexpectedly, sick parade the next morning was a horrible affair, providing reflections on the effects of generosity towards Zoo inmates too seldom touched upon by the press or television.

Despite the fact that, drawing on bitter experience, we had dosed our charges liberally with salts before the start of and during the holiday, the sick list was quite appalling. Many of the animals required minor medical treatment, and some were so ill that they had to be brought into hospital.

But although the toll exacted by the 'sentimentalists' was so heavy, worse – far worse – was that taken by the savages.

Representatives of this minority had thrown to the animals a 'diet' of the most diabolical kind – a 'diet' of

Unhappy Hippos

Thermos flasks, knives and bottle tops. At the end of all these efforts nine animals were dead – including a llama, a bison and a buffalo.

One sadist had fed his victim a banana that concealed a sharpened knife. Others had found their fun in injuring the wing membranes of 'flying foxes', by applying to them lighted cigarettes. And others, evidently indulging a frustrated desire for satire, spent their time in spitting at the chimps, thus eloquently illustrating the link between Man and Ape.

From such depressing manifestations of the reverse side of what so often has been depicted as 'a nation of animal lovers', we all turned with relief to the example set by a young girl, who had travelled four hundred miles to get medical advice for her pet.

*

I encountered the little girl when I walked over to the hospital theatre after a visit to the dens and saw her waiting with her father outside my office door.

She was sitting there very patiently – well-brushed, well scrubbed, and in her Sunday best. She looked both shy and prim, as little girls often do, and on her knees was perched a small box with air-holes bored in it. On enquiry I found that her local veterinary surgeon had recommended her to call on the out-patients' department. Perhaps we could do something to help her pet white mouse?

'So what's wrong with him?' I asked.

'He's got a swelling in the tummy.'

When I took the box from the child and examined its sick inmate – surely one of the smallest white mice ever to be seen – I found that she was right to be concerned. The 'swelling' was an abdominal tumour which, if neglected,

First Catch Your Tiger

might prove fatal. Its best chance lay in an operation, which should be immediate. 'But before I do anything,' I said, 'I had better explain the difficulties . . .'

As regards the degree of surgical skill entailed, the operation would be a fairly straightforward affair, but the danger lay in the stress it might impose on the patient. It would affect its metabolism, and perhaps result in congestive heart failure. The mouse needed an operation I explained to my visitor, and we would do our best for it: but I wanted to be sure that she understood the risks.

For a few moments the little girl soberly considered the matter, and then decided – very courageously – to let the operation proceed. She wanted, she said, to give her mouse a *chance*. It was a decision that – happily – was amply justified by the event.

The dangers that could have arisen failed to materialise and the operation was remarkably free of complications. We removed the tumour without difficulty, and the glow of pleasure in the child's eyes when we returned her pet to her, and it promptly showed its fitness by running up her arm and on to her shoulder, was indeed a rich reward for the problems entailed. But what made the occasion a truly memorable one for me was the discovery that my visitors had come all the way from Cornwall.

It transpired that the little girl had been so upset by the plight of her pet that her father had decided to take time off for the journey. The mouse, he explained, had originally cost only sixpence: but it had come to mean the world to his daughter. He would have been 'a poor sort of father' if he had not tried to help!

Well, goodness knows what the illness of that sixpenny mouse had cost the man in purely material terms . . . terms of fares, lost wages and loss of time . . . but, measured against the happiness of his child, and her confidence in her parents, one is sure that he felt the expenditure was worthwhile.

*

I once went on record as saying – and was taken to task because of it – that ideally not a penny should go to charities devoted to the care or preservation of wild animals while a single child in Britain existed in desperate need. Our loyalties were primarily due to our own species.

I also made plain my feelings towards those so-called animal-lovers to whom a battered child is apparently of less account than, say, an ill-treated kitten. To me such an attitude was – and is – a perversion of the natural order.

How then, I was asked by one of my critics, did I reconcile my opinions with my career? If I did not 'love' animals, how could I attend to their needs? Love is for man.

The very fact that such questions were raised is, in my view, symptomatic of the sloppiness and false sentiment that is generated among people today on the subject of animals, their status and their feelings.

One does not have to 'love' a creature in order to feel a regard for it, and have an interest in its behaviour and characteristics. One does not have to be swayed by sickly sentiment before one can feel responsible for – and towards – a creature in captivity.

Similarly, in decrying the current 'worship' of domestic pets, one can still like their company, and appreciate the ways in which they benefit the family. In fact, were it possible in the social conditions of our age, I would urge that every child be permitted to have a pet of their own. A pet can give a child its first lessons in responsibility, and teach it that, throughout adult life, it will have duties to others smaller or more defenceless than itself.

As a boy, I used to creep downstairs at night to bathe the battle-scars of our mongrel dog 'Pat', a heroic fighter whose disadvantage was that he always selected as adversary the largest dog in the village. Two or three years earlier I had braved my parents' wrath – not to mention pneumonia! while still in my pyjamas – by taking a hot water bottle from the house to my pet rabbit. But I do not think there was anything unduly 'soft' or falsely sentimental about my behaviour: presumably I felt I had a duty to fulfil to those placed in my charge.

Thus when the little girl brought me her white mouse for treatment, I was impressed by the care and concern she had shown towards her pet: but I was even more impressed by the father's concern for his daughter. Each of the pair had acted very commendably, but it was quite impossible to equate these attitudes as stemming from the same motive. In the one case there was the acquired spirit of protectiveness that comes to one when a relatively defenceless creature is associated with the family circle. In the other, the source of inspiration was a father's instinctive love for his daughter, and his understanding of how she felt and thought.

Even my own feelings – over the success of the subsequent operation – were based much more on sympathy for a fellow human than on my natural pleasure (and pleasure it always is) at having alleviated the sufferings of a patient. Glad for the sake of the mouse, and glad professionally as well, my prime concern was for the mouse's owner. I had made a child happy, and I knew just *why* she was happy: I could share in her emotions, and thus sympathise with them. But the psychological processes of the white mouse are something which the white mouse keeps entirely to itself. It is something in which I can have no part or share. The only sensations common to the species are those of pain and fear.

We are deluded when we seek to apply such terms as 'love' to our feelings for animals. Love is a term employed by homo sapiens to express the feelings of like for like. Love – like sympathy – needs reciprocity. An animal knows no love, except in its primitive sense – the love, among some categories, of a mother for its young. No animal feels 'sympathy' for another.

To seek to identify oneself too closely with a different species is to invite disappointment. Worse, it can even lead to anthropomorphic tendencies, while animals can themselves suffer from too close an association with man. Bearing his imprint, they can cease to identify with their own, as in the case of Chi-Chi and An-An.

12. Panda - Monium

On a bitter cold afternoon in March 1966 a battered single decker bus pulled up outside a cage in Moscow Zoo; a plank was tilted from its tailboard and workers started to manhandle a huge crate along it to the ground. Then, suddenly, their burden slipped and hit corner-wise the piled bank of hardened snow. From the interior of the crate arose animal howls denoting terror and rage.

Such was the distressing start of Chi-Chi the panda's first visit to An-An, an episode that, then hailed as likely to make zoological history, and publicised as such in the press of five continents, was to resolve itself into a gallant failure.

Those familiar with Chi-Chi and her habits had anticipated difficulties from the moment the project was first broached.

Far from being a lusty product of the wild, hungering for a mate of her own kind, our panda had become so conditioned to the zoo environment and the company of man, that she had developed anthropomorphic tendencies and, when in season, had even tried to make herself attractive to her embarrassed head keeper!

The trouble was that ever since she was six months old, when she was captured by a Chinese collecting team and taken to Peking Zoo, Chi-Chi had never seen another member of her species, and had become steadily orientated to human company.

Panda – Monium

Thus, before her journey to Moscow, we were kept busy trying to educate her to face the shock of meeting a male of her species by hanging a mirror on the wall of her den, and making sure her pool was always full and reflecting her image.

That way, we reasoned, she could gradually get used to what a panda looked like – what she, *herself*, looked like – but without such aids she might identify herself as being similar in shape to the people around her!

Other difficulties were also envisaged by us as likely to stand in the way of a successful mating, and arose from reasons that were both physical and temperamental. But before recalling these little-publicised snags it is as well to take a look at the circumstances that led up to what should have been a 'zoological' situation becoming so complicated by considerations of scientific interest, experimental necessity, professional prestige and international politics, that the wonder of the Chi-Chi and An-An project lies not in its failure, but in the fact that it was ever attempted.

To the zoologist, the panda has the attraction of being an animal that is not only extraordinarily rare in terms of numbers, but is almost unique in respect of its physical attributes and qualities.

Spending half of the year in the bamboo forests in the mountains of Eastern Tibet and the Szechuan province of China, and descending to the plains when the heavy weather sets in, the panda is remarkable for its dietic variations – made possible by its unusual digestive tract – and in captivity enjoys a variety of food ranging from bamboo shoots, rice and bananas, to chicken and wholemeal bread. It is also remarkable for possessing a modified thumb – somewhat akin to the dog's long-disused 'dew claw'

First Catch Your Tiger

– which it uses to grasp the bamboo, its basic diet in the wild.

To the general public, however, the panda's most endearing quality stems from the peculiar effect created by its head-markings, in particular the black patches on the fur around its eyes. This gives it, very deceptively, a goggly but benevolent appearance, and serves to build up its 'image' as amiable and cuddlesome.

To say that it is neither, but is as piggy-eyed and mean-minded as the grisliest of bears, and just about as ungracious – is almost to lay oneself open to accusations of heresy. So successful has been the P.R. exercise that has made this sluggish, short-sighted and somewhat timid heavyweight into one of the best-loved family favourites in the Zoo that even the Wild Life Trust has adopted it as its emblem!

Another great attraction of the panda lies in the fact that the female of the species occasionally carries, as a woman does, its baby in its arms. Few people have seen a panda doing this – how can they when the animal is so rare? – but practically everyone *knows* about this endearing trait, and it is no accident that the animal is most popular with the ladies.

And yet, strangely enough, the public's affection for the panda is of recent growth, and its 'discovery' by the West is comparatively recent, too: the animal's existence becoming known to Europeans less than a century ago, when Missionary Father David saw panda skins in a Chinese farm-house, and secured some of them so that they could be examined in Paris.

It was not until 1936 that the first living specimen of the species to be obtained by a Westerner – Mrs Ruth Harkness, the American animal collector – was brought into captivity. The London Zoo's first panda, the famous Ming, arrived in

1938, and the acquisition of Chi-Chi twenty years later owed more to accident than design.

Commissioned by an American zoo to trade African animals for a panda, Heini Demmer, an Austrian, based on Nairobi, found the deal baulked by the extension of the Cold War to the Far East when the United States broke off diplomatic relations with China.

At that time Demmer had just effected his 'swap' – obtaining the baby Chi-Chi in the process. His American market having vanished, he decided that the best hope of re-couping his losses lay in his touring European zoos with the animal: and this he did, with considerable effect.

It was as a result of this visit that Chi-Chi came to Britain, and was promptly purchased for the London Zoo. The price, to which Lord Bernstein contributed very substantially, was never disclosed, but it is thought to have been in the region of £10,000.

From the very start of her stay with us, Chi-Chi was something of a problem child. On the other hand – like other problem children – she could claim the defence of being thoroughly misunderstood.

When originally examined by a member of the Zoo staff, the panda the world was later to look to as a mother whose fertility might save her stock from extinction was identified as a male!

It was much later, when she was fully adult, that her behaviour pattern began to provide indications that this assessment was at variance with the facts. It was observed that at certain periods of the year she became faddy, less reliable, and showed symptoms of being 'in season'. She was noticeably attracted towards her keeper, and at times appeared to be trying to make herself attractive to him! A re-think was needed...

First Catch Your Tiger

Another theory that came under review was the one responsible for consigning our panda to the 'bear group' in the Zoo. *Was* a panda truly a bear? Some of us did not think so. But if a panda was not a bear, then to which family did it belong?

It was not until April 1964 that we had our first real chance to put such questions to the test, and get a positive confirmation, or denial, of our doubts by conducting a really scientific examination.

The occasion arose when Chi-Chi developed an eye infection, and was taken to the hospital for treatment. As the operation would of course require the animal to be anaesthetised, we decided that it offered us an opportunity for investigation into both sex and type that had hitherto been denied us. The results of this decision were truly sensational.

There was a big audience in the operating theatre when Chi-Chi, suitably narcotised, was lifted on to the table. The occasion was an important one; historically and scientifically its significance was of great interest. For the first time a giant panda was to be anaesthetised, and treated by the techniques of modern surgery. However, in addition to the interest it evoked among veterinary and zoological circles there were factors involved in the affair that were to endow it with heavy political overtones. Incredibly there were signs that the determination of Chi-Chi's sex might become an international *cause célèbre* . . .

Some while previously, Sir Solly Zuckerman, who was then the Government's Chief Scientific Adviser, had visited Russia for the discussion preluding the nuclear test agreement. While there, he had been able to renew his acquaint-

Panda – Monium

ance – as Secretary of London Zoo – with personalities of Moscow Zoo and had become interested in a 'Russian' panda – the celebrated An-An.

An-An had arrived in Moscow from Peking a few years earlier, and soon the talk had turned to the possibilities of mating. To confirm Chi-Chi's sex had become an urgent priority!

Sir Solly knew all about our tacit 're-classification' of Chi-Chi's sexual status, but positive proof would be tactful before the Moscow Zoo could consider the most tentative arrangements. Could we get really positive results, and prove them? If we could, then a truly dramatic situation might develop, a joint East–West effort to save an endangered species.

The situation was complicated by the fact that, as a giant panda had never before been subjected to anaesthesia, we had no indication as to the quantity or type of agent that would be required, but eventually we based our calculations on the 'dosage' which we had previously administered to a bear.

First we narcotised Chi-Chi with phencylidine and promazine. Next we intubated her, and then we anaesthetised her with a mixture of lalothane, nitrous oxide and oxygen. This regime proved to be extremely effective, and the operation on the eye which was relatively simple was carried out, with no 'incident' to mar its success. But of course the eye operation was in some respects of minor importance when compared with our other aims of exploration and discovery.

It was therefore with tremendous satisfaction and relief that we were able to confirm the true sex of our patient; and then, for the benefit of our Russian colleagues, provide our findings with a visual proof.

First Catch Your Tiger

Our 'British' panda's claim to feminity was now established beyond all possible doubt!

*

The confirmation of Chi-Chi's sex was one thing, but the classification – and public disclosure – of her family group was quite another.

During the operation, we had taken blood and tissue samples from our patient in order to establish her chromosome pattern, and see whether or not it fitted into that of the bear group, to which, until then, she had been deemed to belong. This way, we felt, we could resolve once and for all the controversy that was so exercising our colleagues, and establish whether or not the animal was unique in its origins and descent.

Alas for such optimism!

The chromosome counts – when compared with similar samples taken from 'known bears' not only showed that our doubts about the panda seemed well founded: they also appeared to prove that certain of those 'bears' had counts that were unlike other bears! It seemed the Linnean classification, based on fine anatomical and other identifying features was at difference with our results. Our investigations had been successful.

Unfortunately, however, it soon became apparent that our investigation had been *too* successful – too successful by half!

We had found the panda more akin to the racoon than to the bear, and therefore requiring a new tag. But if we were to re-classify the panda, then what should be done about the other so-called 'bears'? If chromosome counts were to be given a significant authority in classification, then not only the panda but the other deviationists must be re-labelled

Panda – Monium

too! The thought of this appalled everyone and the project, though doubtless it will be reviewed in due course, was dropped like a hot potato!

After this there arose controversy over the best way of exploiting Chi-Chi's newly discovered sexual attributes, and some of us found ourselves somewhat opposed to the official view, subscribed to by both the British and Russian authorities, that the animals should conform to established standards and procreate as the result of physical contact. Why – we asked – could not a less fallible method be adopted? Why should we not resort to artificial insemination?

To us, the official plan seemed a little wearisome, and complex. We knew little about the panda's pattern of sex behaviour, but what we did know tended to identify the animal as an isolationist, seldom cohabiting with its mate, and coming into season for a fairly short period of the year. Thus the idea of putting together two of the species – complete strangers to each other, and uprooted by man from their natural surroundings – in the hope that they would have successful sex, struck us as something of a gamble.

It was with such considerations in mind that I decided to write to Igor Sosnovski, the Director of Moscow Zoo, and once more reverted to the possible advantages offered by A.I.

I had established good relations with the Russian when he had made a visit to London, and had found him to be well endowed with professional expertise and, apparently, a fairly flexible outlook. But, this notwithstanding, our hint met with little response.

This may have been due to the fact that Moscow shared the view expressed by our own authorities, namely, that the complications in extracting the sperm from a male panda might prove dangerous to the donor. Equally, it could have been due to the Russians believing as our own people believed, that we should know more about the timing of ovulation in the panda before attempting A.I. But, although we found these attitudes disappointing, our minds were soon preoccupied with bigger problems. It seemed that the prospects of even the planned exchange had begun to dim...

It had been in 1962 when Sir Solly had first raised the subject, in the form of a letter to Moscow's Academy of Sciences. When he had made his on-the-spot appeal, a full year of intermittent discussions had elapsed, and then more time had passed before we obtained our final proof of Chi-Chi's sex.

All through this period, the Russians' reactions to the zoological implications of the pandas' mating had been enthusiastic, but their responses to suggestions as to how this could take place had been equivocal, to say the least. They had made it known that they were reluctant to send An-An to London – an attitude probably contributed to by reasons of prestige – while we were equally adverse to sending Chi-Chi to Moscow, in view of the rigours of the Russian winter.

It was later hoped that a meeting could be arranged at some point conveniently placed between the two cities, but when this suggestion was tentatively advanced, the Russians neatly riposted by suggesting East Berlin!

Understandably this had aroused no enthusiasm on our side of the Wall, and eventually we were back to where we started. But even when our own Zoo authorities, anxious to break the deadlock agreed that the venue should be Moscow, the matter was not decided.

At one time An-An was sick, at another there were difficulties over diet, at another doubts were cast on the male panda's virility – somehow or other the Russians always seemed to produce excuses whenever the attempt was made to transform their declarations of intent into any sort of purposeful action.

The reason for this apparent havering on Moscow's part has never been thoroughly explained. However, looking back, I feel that it was probably based on fears for their panda's safety. Chi-Chi and An-An had been isolated for so long from their kind, and so much conditioned to the company of man, that there were apprehensions as regarding their reactions to each other. Say they should fight, and suffer serious injury?

Chi-Chi, as we knew from experience, was highly temperamental, and so domesticated that we had had to 'educate' her even to recognise her own identity, so thoroughly had she been imprinted with man. Yet now, inevitably, we were to take this timid animal from her quarters, transport her to a spot fifteen hundred miles away, confront her with new lodgings in an inhospitable climate, and then subject her to the sexual advances – if he made any! – of a male panda as imprinted by man as herself! Small wonder, perhaps, that we regarded the outcome of the exercise with somewhat less than minimal confidence.

With so many discouraging factors playing their part to mar this originally optimistic attempt at East–West cooperation, we became sceptical of the chances of the pandas ever meeting – let alone the prospects of that meeting being successful. And when, following further delay, it was suddenly announced that the Russians had sanctioned the project, and we were fixing a date for Chi-Chi's

First Catch Your Tiger

visit, our feelings were divided between relief and scepticism.

*

Whatever else may change in modern society, the fact that 'half a loaf is better than none', remains as true as ever, and thus, although we still entertained our preferences for the A.I. technique, and were not unduly hopeful of success for the coming confrontation, we felt that at least it was better to attempt it than to do nothing at all.

It was in early 1966, when Desmond Morris, as Curator of Mammals, hastened to Moscow to conclude the details of the deal, and make the necessary arrangements for our 'British' panda's reception. Chi-Chi, it was eventually decided, would start her long-delayed journey in March with Sam Morton, her head keeper, and myself to act as escorts.

Such was the start of an affair that, inspired initially by the belief that it was in the best interests of zoology, was to end up as a mixture of frustration and weariness. In doing so it was to provide the press with a field day.

13. Moon Over Moscow

The first snag in our plans for Chi-Chi occurred when it was found that the smooth running prestigious Comet that had originally been offered for her transport could not accommodate the crate in which she was to be confined during the flight. The access hatches were too small.

Showing the greatest willingness to help, B.E.A. then made the wonderful gesture of scrapping their Comet flight and offering us a different aircraft, the Vanguard. This proved to be an excellent alternative, though there was the disadvantage that it was distinctly noisier than our first choice, and we were somewhat apprehensive lest this should upset our panda's delicate nerves.

By then my own nerves were somewhat over-taxed.

Even at the best of times the task of moving a very rare, extremely highly-strung wild animal by air is not exactly problem-free – not if one is conscientious about its health and comfort. But when the animal is the cynosure of the world's communications industry, and its every move is faithfully reported to an audience totalling hundreds of millions in publications ranging from the *Cleveland Free Trader* to *Isvestia* and *The Times of India*, the path of the prodigy's escort is beset by a thousand pitfalls.

From the very start of the operation one was acutely conscious that, however pure might be the motives of the London and Moscow Zoo authorities in initiating it, what

First Catch Your Tiger

had started as an experiment in zoology and conservation had come to acquire strong overtones of politics.

But even the not altogether uncomplicated reflections aroused in us by the considerations of this aspect of the visit, had to take second place to the resolving of the technical innovations required by the panda's transit.

Carried at varying altitudes, and exposed to varying pressures, Chi-Chi would be moved in a matter of hours from her snug accommodation in the temperate zone and delivered to a completely alien – and therefore suspect – environment held in the frozen grip of the Russian winter. How best could we meet the problems of health and morale that such a dramatic switch would naturally entail?

Nor was the question of her reactions 'on delivery' – the only one that would need to be resolved: there was the problem of her behaviour during the journey itself. What effect would aircraft noise and vibration have upon the sensitive passenger? Would the cabin temperatures and humidity that had proved so acceptable to humans affect her adversely? Here we had a mammal, coated in thick fur. Might there not be danger of her over-heating? If there was, might she not panic?

In view of such factors, it was obvious that the amenities required to maintain Chi-Chi in good condition during the flight would have to be considerably in excess of those afforded by the type of restraint box employed by the hospital. Accordingly, in cooperation with the Zoo's Clerk of Works, we devoted much time and mental agitation to the shape and nature of the panda's temporary living quarters; a cross between a crate and a mobile den that was far in advance of anything hitherto produced for the safety and comfort of a creature in transit.

First emphasis on the design for Chi-Chi's abode was

laid-on air conditioning. Many variable vents were provided in the top of the box, consisting of air-holes with swivel cups, while the ends of the box were so contrived that they could be slid back, thus allowing draught to be admitted – or excluded – between the framework of iron bars. There had been some suggestion of using ice blocks to keep our companion even cooler, but this had turned out to be too messy a process to please the aircraft's owners, so instead of this we directed at the crate the cool air nozzles on the Vanguard's overhead rack.

By the time we had finished with its construction, and the painters had brightly decorated it in the smart livery of B.E.A., the crate was a really impressive looking affair, But by then we were considering other matters that were relevant to the panda's safety in flight.

We believed that the ventilation of Chi-Chi's crate would be efficient enough to prevent her over-heating, but we could not be sure. We knew that the strength of the crate was such as to keep the animal in confinement, however great might be her rage or fright, but we could not guarantee that it would prevent her doing herself an injury. So what should be done to further minimise the risk?

The argument hinged principally on whether or not the panda should be sedated; and on this we were fairly evenly divided. Some argued that sedation would be necessary to keep the animal quiet, and thus prevent her from falling, or battering herself violently against the bars. But others took the view that sedation would defeat its object, by increasing the risk of over-heating. I, myself, subscribed to this latter theory.

Sedatives can be unsuitable if used on a patient who is stimulated by noise. In fact they can lead to greater stress than that prevailing in the unsedated. Certain tranquillisers cause sedation *until* stimulation of the patient, when violent, short-lived episodes of panic can occur with all the consequent overtones of self-injury or – at the worst – escape.

The departure of Chi-Chi for Moscow was made with considerable pomp, and was preceded by the sort of detailed planning that was later to evoke from the press such heady descriptions as 'a military operation'.

Shortly before Departure Day (11th March, 1968), a conference was called at the Zoo to which were invited all those most directly concerned in the V.I.P. flight. From services and supply officers of B.E.A. to Zoo officials, there were no fewer than seventeen people at this prolonged briefing, and much useful ground was covered. Introducing ourselves to each other, we compared notes about our duties – and the panda's requirements – and then took a thoughtful look at the passenger herself. Big decisions were made as a result of our discussions – B.E.A. obligingly agreeing to take out more than thirty seats in order that the crate could be more satisfactorily secured. Nor had the minutiae of the enterprise been neglected, the stewardess being assured that Chi-Chi could be allowed the odd bar or so of chocolate. In fact, by the end of the briefing, the only thing remaining unrehearsed was the confrontation to which all its efforts had been directed.

On the day itself the journey from Regent's Park to Heathrow lived up to the 'military' analogy noted earlier. We assembled at an unearthly hour – before first light! – to get our final briefing, and then travelled in convoy, with one car spearheading the path of the vehicle carrying the crated – but curious – Chi-Chi, and another forming an escort to the rear. Public participation was soon evident, however, to a degree rarely associated with 'military' occasions. Despite the hour, well-wishers thronged the airport, and a general air of carnival prevailed, to mock our dead seriousness.

Over the weeks, public interest in what was to be publicised as 'Operation Panda' – though *not* by the London Zoo – had escalated to the stage where attitudes towards the anticipated copulation were to be summed up by one writer: 'The Anthropomorphs have had their picnic*.' To other observers the project had 'Chauvinistic' touches, and, to a certain extent, this was true. 'What a pity our British panda had to be the female of the pair,' I heard one ostensibly sensible citizen regretfully reflect – the prestige of Flag and Phallic symbolism obviously being interchangeable. But of course the majority of those whose attention had been focused on the panda project represented shades of opinion that were far less extreme. To these people and to the press, its attractiveness lay in the fact that it seemed quite a lark.

Among items of equipment accompanying Chi-Chi's crate, was a set of transparent plastic panels. When the box ends and bars were removed, these could be slipped into place, and the animal photographed without being exposed to draughts and weather. Needless to say that our star was 'shot' over and over again.

Next came the turn of the Vanguard's captain – John Corbishley – to stand before the cameras; after which Sally Morton, who was accompanying her husband on the trip with their three year old son, became the centre of the photographers' attention. All in all the start of the historic mission was quite a party.

To this massive invasion of their privacy and calm, Chi-Chi's fellow passengers reacted with some surprise, but with no visible disapproval. It was, one businessman said,

* Katherine Whitehorn, *Observer*, 6th Nov. 1968.

First Catch Your Tiger

'a bit of a giggle'. Nor, despite our worries about the effect on our charge of so much excitement, did Chi-Chi show signs of being much the worse.

She was naturally restless – my diary records that at one stage she was scraping the floor of her cage, and kicking, but she accepted bamboo shoots, even though she ate them nervously. In fact, for most of the time she appeared to be extraordinarily complacent.

When the last farewell had been said, and the engines had started up, she surprised us all by nonchalantly resting her feet on the bars. And then, when the Vanguard at last began to climb, this astonishing animal raised herself to a sitting position, jammed her hind legs and bottom against the bars, and relaxed like a veteran.

The weak sunshine of early spring was bathing the airport buildings as we took our last look at Heathrow. Noisy and irreverent but thoroughly good-natured, the farewell London had given us was to form a memorable contrast to the scene at our destination.

Snow . . . We encountered the first flakes when over the Polish border, and, as the aircraft began to lose height for the long approach to Moscow, there was a sharp drop in the cabin temperature, and a slight shudder down the spine. Throughout the four hours that had elapsed since take-off Chi-Chi had been a model of decorum. True that at one stage she had been irritated by a fresh photo session and had struck out at a cameraman, but, in general, she had kept extraordinarily calm. However, I now noticed signs of restlessness, and these were soon transformed into aggression. Angrily she again lashed out at the photographers before relapsing into yet another series of the extraordinary manoeuvres we had noticed on take-off; and which she adapted to adjust herself to each new phase of the flight.

It was when we landed, however, that the panda's real troubles began. No sooner had the Vanguard cut engines and come to a stop, than the aircraft was enveloped by a horde of officials, most of them members of the brown-uniformed airport police. Within seconds they were checking, questioning, and generally pushing us around, and then in a general confusion – almost impossible to describe – a group of workmen arrived and took possession of Chi-Chi!

The aircraft carried a landing ramp that had been specially designed to ensure the smooth handling of the panda's 'den', but the Russians completely ignored this civilised innovation. Without a 'by your leave' from anyone, and deaf to all queries and protests, a group of them unlashed the crate, dragged it across the floor, and humped it, none too gently, on to a cross-legged fork lift – And then they promptly drove off!

To say that we were surprised at these proceedings would be a masterpiece of understatement. Carried out, with astonishing speed, they made a picture that was so unlike anything we had been led to expect that we were literally stupefied.

Viewed in retrospect, the incident certainly had its humorous aspect, but this was not very apparent at the time. The contrast between this Slavonic version of the hi-jack, and the red-carpet treatment our charge had received in London, upset us, and the aftermath brought little in the way of reassurance.

At last allowed to leave the aircraft, and seething with impatience to find out what had happened to Chi-Chi, we searched vainly for transport – then gave up and made our

First Catch Your Tiger

way to the airport buildings on foot accompanied by Igor Sosnovski. Nobody seemed to know – or care – anything about us, but of course there was in any case a complete language barrier. As we trudged, heavily burdened, across the frozen snow, the wind from the Steppes howled around our numbed ears, and stretched its icy fingers into our bones. For a brief moment I was reminded of those dramatic – and depressing – portraits of the retreat of 1812!

Even when – to our intense relief – we at last caught sight of the 'kidnapped' Chi-Chi scant attention was paid to our *amour propre* as escorts. The animal had been loaded on to the back of what was by London standards a shabby and dilapidated single-decker bus, from whence it was directing the most heartfelt protests! By then we had been welcomed by our Moscow colleague, Igor Sosnovski, but even his presence seemed to make little difference – and no sooner had we arrived than the Russians drove off at speed, parking on the most distant part of the apron.

Only then did anyone have a word to throw to us, and we were taken under the protective wing of Toya Sokolova, an attractive blonde, who spoke perfect English with a strong American accent. She not only served to brighten the scene a little but helped to explain the apparent snatch. The bus, she explained, belonged to the Moscow Zoo.

Miss Sokolova was certainly not the type of girl to let the ice melt under her feet. Once in the airport buildings we were rushed into a small office, where we were promptly presented with an enormous bill. The rent for our hotel rooms, they explained – payable strictly in advance!

No sooner had we settled this than it was time for customs' clearance. After this we were ushered into separate cars; Sam's leaving first, reportedly for the Zoo.

Still not fully recovered from the effects of the initial

Moon Over Moscow

confusion, and still prey to apprehension for the well being of our panda, I suggested to Toya that I followed Sam's example. 'Let's go straight to the Zoo.' But, when we got there, it was to encounter yet another of the 'misunderstandings' that were to bedevil our stay. Sam had already been deposited at the hotel!

Finally, to cap everything, and put a suitably sombre seal on the events of the day, came Chi-Chi's rude manhandling from the Zoo bus. It was dark by then, and as the crate hit the ground, its unfortunate prisoner gave vent to cries of anguish and rage!

The obvious unhappiness occasioned our panda during the first hours of her visit to Moscow had I am sure historic consequences. The stress that resulted certainly set the pattern of her behaviour for well over a week, and that week was critical in the breeding programme. Nor did her transit troubles end with her unceremonious unloading.

Her crate was humped on to a primitive iron trolley for transport to her new quarters, and then bumped along an uneven frozen path. At the end of this, it had to be manhandled sideways, through a gap in the fence, into one of the outside paddocks; and then pushed up a steep mound that formed part of the entrance area to the inside cages. Nor surprisingly, the journey did not improve our panda's morale, a fact that she advertised in tones that all could understand.

From having been so calm and comfortable in the aircraft, Chi-Chi was by this time reduced to a state of near-hysteria – come to think of it, I felt a little hysterical myself. The cries of the animal rose both loud and clear.

'Somehow I must free her from the crate – and free her fast,' I thought.

It was then – and only then – that I realised, with sicken-

First Catch Your Tiger

ing frustration, that the absentee Sam had gone off with the key!

A concerned audience of Zoo officials, mustered in the snow as a sort of reception committee, uttered helpful suggestions, including an offer to collect my absent friend. By then, however, I had had enough of delays, and for Chi-Chi's sake – and the sake of my own shattered nerves – could wait no longer.

I 'opened the box' by breaking the locks with a crowbar. Desperate diseases so often need desperate remedies . . .

*

Despite what were often the most frustrating circumstances, I was able to develop during the Moscow stay a sincere liking and respect for our Russian colleagues, and I have reason to believe that this sentiment was reciprocated.

Sosnovski, the Director of the Moscow Zoo, was a very dedicated zoologist, and most eager to cooperate in making our enterprise a success. In a different, but very important sphere of influence, we found in M. Nemov, An-An's keeper, a very valuable ally. Most helpful at all times, Nemov had a wealth of wisdom regarding the animal world and was as devoted as Morton to his particular charge.

But much though we might like our opposite numbers – both as individuals, and partners in a project of mutual interest – we were poles apart in our view of everyday life and politics, and this became more apparent for every day that passed.

For example, there was Sosnovski's attitude towards the press.

In Britain, we had achieved coexistence with the newspapers, and this had often blossomed into cooperation, mutually beneficial. In Russia, the Western press's attitude

Chi-Chi is introduced to her travelling quarters.

Chi-Chi meets her pilot and hostess.

With Igor Sosnovski, Director of Moscow Zoo, walking from the plane after arrival.

Chi-Chi's Russian quarters.

Chi-Chi at London Zoo.

A final, equally unsuccessful, attempt to mate Chi-Chi and An-An.

towards the panda – and most other things too – was considered to be 'frivolous' and even 'obstructive', and this led to some strain in our own relationships with the newsmen.

For example, the Western photographers who had travelled with us, wanted to record Chi-Chi's arrival in Moscow; so, too, did Russian photographers gathered on the Tarmac. But Sosnovski would have none of it, and promptly intervened with a ban! 'This,' he said, 'is a serious scientific experiment in the mating of giant pandas. All this publicity is frivolous and unnecessary.' As guests, we naturally had to abide by our host's decision which was irrevocable. In fact we later heard that one reason for Chi-Chi's swift transit to the Zoo was to ensure the ban's effectiveness.

It seemed odd to us that scientists who believed in – or at least acquiesced in – the most distorted reportage and comment on the political scene, should be so nicely puritanical when it came to the press's treatment of the technical and biological; but we kept our thoughts to ourselves.

Yet as regards the willingness of the Russians to provide for the panda's health and comfort we had very little to complain about – except that they did not always see eye to eye with us on how this could best be done.

To start with, our opposite numbers were no great believers in the value of fresh air, and were amazed when I asked that the exercise paddock – five foot deep in snow! – should be cleared to enable Chi-Chi to take a walk. They took quite a bit of convincing before they agreed to the move, being fearful of our panda catching cold. Again, there were differences of attitude towards what constituted the best diet for the animal; with An-An being a terrific

First Catch Your Tiger

enthusiast for porridge and Russian bread, Chi-Chi's disgusted rejection of such fare gave her the reputation of being 'faddy'. But these troubles, too, were ironed out, and Sam was given the facilities to provide our panda with the sort of food that pleased her Westernised palate.

However, the morning after her ill-starred introduction to Moscow, found Chi-Chi still tremendously upset, and Morton and I were quite unable to soothe her. In fact, for all the good we did, we might just as well have remained back home – in our austere rooms in the Hotel Metropole, dubbed – very misleadingly – the Claridge's of Moscow.

For the sight of us, as we walked around the perimeter of her house, only served to aggravate her self-pity, and turn it into fury. She slashed at us with her claws, barking and howling. She rubbed her vulva on her sleeping board. And occasionally she performed a curious 'marking' trick that I had seen for the first time in London when her crate had been shown her. Standing close to the front of the cage, and parallel to it, she raised one hind leg vertically above the other, and presented her vulva to the bars.

In one sense the visit was a depressing one: in another it added urgency to our worries by supporting an uneasy suspicion that was forming in my mind. Not only was the animal feeling miserable, very probably she was also rapidly going off-season!

We had guessed that the oestrus – the short-lived physiological state of sexual activity when female animals are ready to receive a male and conceive – was of even shorter duration than usual when related to pandas. Had it been shortened still more by Chi-Chi's current distress? Had it – dreadful thought – been impaired altogether?

Dismissing the last possibility as a not very helpful one, I considered the first and came to these conclusions:

1. With time the essence, it was imperative that the animals should be put together without delay.
2. To effect this the quarantine period must be drastically curtailed.

These points I then put to Sosnovski who appeared to be in complete agreement with me, but his subsequent warning that only 'the very highest authorities' could sanction such a move proved all too accurate.

Despite our joint efforts, and frequent references to a clean bill of health supplied by the London Zoo, ten days elapsed before an officialdom that did everything by the book at last relented. In the meanwhile our panda's health and temper had deteriorated still further, changing from bad to worse, and what influence we'd had on her appeared to have dissipated.

On the 14th, Chi-Chi allowed Sam Morton – greatly daring – to scratch her back, but far from being mollified by this gesture of affection had replied to it only with a fit of angry barking.

By the 15th she was attacking everyone in sight; and I settled down to recording in my diary the following gloomy prophecy:

'I do not think Chi-Chi is in oestrus.'

As I wrote, the Moscow night was at its gloomiest. The snow was falling heavily, and my thoughts strayed back to my visit in the afternoon when I had insisted on the drifts being cleared from Chi-Chi's paddock so that she could get exercise. This had caused Sosnowski great alarm, and he had added, surprisingly, that An-An never went out in the winter.

Thanks to the alien environment, and the stress it imposed upon her I was convinced by then that Chi-Chi's

First Catch Your Tiger

œstrus had come to a sudden end. However, I concluded my diary entry with one faint note of cheer. Sam had reported that our charge was barking oddly – and the sound was not unlike her bleat noise of œstrus.

Alas, there was to be no more bleating to sustain our hopes in the days to come.

14. To Mate or Not to Mate?

It was not until the 24th – after my return from a consultation in London – that the quarantine bar on Chi-Chi was eventually lifted. The immediate sequel, when we allowed the animals to sniff at each other through the bars of their dens was scarcely encouraging. There was aggressive barking from Chi-Chi, a half-snarl from An-An, and mutually 'threatening gestures' including much baring of teeth.

Even when we decided that Thursday the 31st should be the date when the animals would be put together, our belief in the venture's success was at very low ebb, Sosnovski agreeing with me that (to quote my diary of the time): 'there is little if any chance of them mating'. In fact our main purpose in fixing the 31st deadline was 'because at least such an attempt will surely establish the facts from a morass of theory.'

At that same meeting we also reached a tentative verbal agreement on what to do should the attempt fail. Under this arrangement Chi-Chi would stay in Moscow for an attempt later in the year, when observers of the Zoological Society could visit her and, should they so desire, impose hormone therapies to ensure her fertility and sexual activity. Thursday the 31st, if not exactly Now or Never, would at least decide whether the panda project would have to wait until Chi-Chi's next oestrus!

First Catch Your Tiger

The morning of the experiment when we met at 9 a.m. for a final review, the circumstances seemed somewhat brighter than they had been. Chi-Chi had shown no signs of aggression for the past few days, and was relatively quiet. Although she had lost weight, had not eaten at all for four of the nineteen days she had been in Moscow, and had touched very little on the remaining fifteen, she had shown some interest in her morning feed, and generally did not seem as frightened as she had been.

Thus we decided to proceed as planned; first arranging, however, to have a strong force of keepers available, armed with broomsticks and hoses. The job of these men was to separate the pandas should they fight, and very soon it became apparent that their services would be needed.

Of the circumstances that led up to their intervention, my Russian opposite number presented a laconic, but all embracing report, which I now quote, though in truncated style.

      Chi-Chi out at 10 a.m.
10.05 Has sniffed tree where An-An marked.
10.15 An-An to be released while Chi-Chi is quiet and not too cold.
10.20 An-An emerges. Cautiously. An-An enters paddock. Chi-Chi still walking around. Mutual staring.
10.25 An-An crossing to Chi-Chi in corner.
      Staring and still.
      An-An retreats to inspect tree stump.
      Licking where Chi-Chi sniffed.
      Marks tree stump.
      Approaches Chi-Chi.
      Promptly attacked Chi-Chi.
      Separated by gun and water and men.

An-An's attack – which was halted only after Sosnovski,

To Mate or Not to Mate?

recovering from 'flu, had been drenched to the skin by a misdirected firehose! – had certainly been no rough attempt at courtship. The immediacy with which he had launched it made it all too plain that his intentions were purely aggressive. He had gripped the unfortunate Chi-Chi by her left hind leg, and rolled her on her back, biting at her abdomen as he did so.

She was screaming when the rescue team eventually beat off her assailant and got her back to her cage. And on examination I found her to be bleeding from a wound in the foot. She could walk normally, but her respirations were rapid and she was suffering from shock. I administered a sedative – acetylpromazine – which I placed in her drinking water, and then I returned to the hotel to work on the final draft of the agreement with the Russians that would leave Chi-Chi in Moscow for a second mating introduction in October. After the events of the morning it was obvious that Chi-Chi was destined for a long, long rest.

At 2.45 I received an urgent phone call to return to the Zoo immediately: there was 'trouble' with our panda. When I arrived there accompanied by Morton, it was to find Chi-Chi staggering about with her eyes closed. She was deeply sedated and inco-ordinate, indicating that she was still very shocked. I was alarmed at her reaction to the day.

Yet our own concern – great though it was – was as nothing compared to that of our flustered hosts, and we began to feel that the agreement itself might be in jeopardy. Quite obviously the Zooparc authorities were now afraid of the responsibility they would have to assume regarding Chi-Chi's health, and certainly her appearance was far from reassuring. Yet even when she began to make a big improvement, and the agreement reached the point of ratification, the great concern of our Russian colleagues was

First Catch Your Tiger

manifest in the questions that they asked us. Would we give them a list of diseases to which pandas were prone? We found this to be ridiculous – they had their own veterinary staff! – but symptomatic of their desire for an insurance policy. And then they expressed their fears about the effect on Chi-Chi of the scorching Moscow summer: how could they ward against this? they demanded. I suggested that blocks of ice, and water sprays if necessary, should be able to keep her reasonably comfortable; but even our promise that should she fall seriously ill we would fly the panda home failed to allay the Russians' apprehensions.

By the 2nd April it was obvious to Morton and myself – and to the Zooparc too – that although Chi-Chi was still somewhat disturbed as a result of An-An's attack, she was basically fit and would soon regain her customary good health: but still the Russians expressed great agitation. What drugs? they asked. What treatment? And what should they do if such and such – or so and so – occurred? Finally, I felt that I could stand this recital no longer, and told them somewhat brusquely, 'For God's sake leave the animal alone!'

Oddly enough, our colleagues appeared to see the point in this, and from then on their alarm was expressed only in *sotto voce*!

It was on April 3rd that we left Moscow to return home, minus Chi-Chi, and make our reports to the Zoo. And, as our aircraft took off, all of us felt a great sense of relief. It was frustrating to leave unfinished the work to which, despite our initial doubts, we had set ourselves with some enthusiasm. But despite the undoubted keenness of our Russian opposite numbers to collaborate to the full in the strictly professional sense, the visit had been a rather exacting one. Except for the hospitality afforded by the kindness

To Mate or Not to Mate?

of certain members of the staff of the British Embassy, together with the Manager of B.E.A. Moscow, Ken Hawkins and his wife, our social life had been nil, and, for the Mortons in particular – with a young child to look after – the disadvantages presented by the weather, the language barrier, and the unfamiliar diet had been formidable.

Again, our visit had coincided with the outbreak of an influenza epidemic which had necessitated us making our (twice or thrice daily) visits to the Zooparc by taxi; this further emphasising our isolation from the average Muscovite, while the cold war's sudden freezing (related to the Gerald Brooke affair) had led to an extra security consciousness in a city that, at the best of times, could scarcely be considered as uninhibited in the welcome it afforded the visiting Westerner.

However, such disadvantages apart, it had been an experience that I do not think I would like to have missed, and one that, despite the failure of our major purpose, had provided links between the professionals of our two great Zoos that no amount of formal correspondence could have achieved on its own.

Just before the aircraft took off, I heard for the umpteenth time the strains of a tune that had greeted us on our arrival and had been repeated every time we switched on the radio set in our hotel rooms – the haunting chords of 'Moon over Moscow'. Local 'top of the pops' its oddly-moving refrain had become a favourite even with us Westerners, and I remember wondering briefly whether, in the softer months to come, the Moscow moon might not favourably influence our 'British' panda's reactions to her exile, and its cause. Would she? Would he? Would *they*? Quite suddenly I discovered that I had almost ceased to care!

15. Zoo-Men's Dilemma

Of the subsequent Moscow meeting of this 'pair of ill-starred lovers' – whose status had become of international interest – I cannot write as an eye-witness, but purely as one with access, through the courtesy of his colleagues, to the narratives of those most involved in the occasion.

By the time that the second mating attempt was due, I had left London Zoo to take up another appointment, and the care of our panda had passed into other hands. But I followed very keenly the story that unfolded – a story that, initially, appeared to be one of hope triumphing over experience, but, alas, concluded with 'hope' taking an extremely nasty knock!

It was on October 3rd that the Zoo's team was alerted by a cablegram from Moscow: Chi-Chi once more appeared to be in season! They flew out the following day, to the momentous news that An-An had started to bleat!

By the 5th excitement was high, and with Sosnovski returning from a visit to Budapest, it was happily recorded that:

'Chi-Chi was seen to present her rear end to An-An for the first time, pressing it against the grille, tail raised.'

And An-An, so it appeared, was 'very interested' in her.

To the London team, enormously encouraged by this manifestation of natural reaction, urgency was the essence

Zoo-Men's Dilemma

of success, and they requested that the animals be immediately put together. Unfortunately this could not be done. Sosnovski would not be able to reach the Zoo until the following afternoon, and many arrangements had to be made; not the least of them being precautions for the animals' security.

The following day, the whole Zoo was closed to the public, and a strong force of keepers stood by, with water hoses, wooden shields and an anaesthetic pistol. High Zoo officials watched the event from concealment, and a barrier of leaves and screens kept even the pressmen – specially selected – from the pandas' vision.

These precautions taken, the animals were put together at 3 p.m. But an hour later the attempt had been written off as yet another failure and the disappointed observers were on their way to tea.

This time it was Chi-Chi who had played the role of spoil-sport. On several occasions, An-An had tried to approach her – only warily to recoil before her barks and blows. In face of such displeasure, his eagerness disappeared, and the day's entry ended on the sombre note that 'he eventually mounted her, but without success.'

The next attempt was made the following day, but this, too, ended in utter failure, with Chi-Chi repulsing every effort of her would-be mate, and seemingly quite regardless of his superior size and weight.

It was then decided to leave the animals together throughout the night – under constant observation from a team of officials drawn from each of the Zoos – but there again, the results were completely fruitless. The Zoo officials stayed wide-awake – while the animals went to sleep!

It was on the 8th when, momentarily, there appeared to be the chance of a successful mating. Provoked by Chi-Chi's continuing resistance, and evidently the prey of intense frustration, An-An abandoned his excessive caution and really tried to assert himself. In a serious mating effort, he charged at Chi-Chi and then evading her frantic bites and blows, he took her by the scruff of her neck and held her down. Alas, this initiative went completely unrewarded. The female just would not respond and kept her tail down. A little later, she drove him back.

This ignominious repulse of An-An's advances was a sad blow to the optimism of its human observers. But later it took an even harder knock, when confronted by the exasperating fact that, sexually, Chi-Chi appeared to be somewhat warped. She seemed to be more attracted to the keeper, and even complete strangers, than she was to the mate that they had chosen for her.

When Nemov entered her cage, to try and push her out into the enclosure, where An-An was waiting, she allowed the Russian to pat her on the back and then – to his intense embarrassment – raised her tail and rear-end in sexual response!

When one of the officials ventured to put his hand between the bars, the same disconcerting symptoms were apparent, Chi-Chi orientating instinctively to the human, even though An-An was only some ten feet away.

When these demonstrations were linked with similar incidents, occurring during the spring attempts, the prospects of successfully mating the pandas dropped to zero, and by the 14th, after two or three last-minute confrontations had proved fruitless, it was agreed that the team – and Chi-Chi herself – should return to London.

*

When anticipating what turned out to be the final episode

Zoo-Men's Dilemma

in this discouraging, though instructive history – namely the attempt made in 1968/69 on Chi-Chi's home ground in London – Sosnovski said in advance that the chance of success was slender, but the experiment would be worth trying. Even with the advantage of hindsight to guide one, it is difficult to quarrel with this thoughtful assessment of the situation or the reluctance of the two Zoos to confess to complete failure before making a further bid to achieve success.

In their epitaph to the Moscow failure, the observing team reached the following conclusions:

'It appears that Chi-Chi's long isolation from other pandas has "imprinted" her sexually on human beings and that, despite (1) Strong sexual motivation (2) Prolonged familiarisation with An-An, and (3) Persistent, non-aggressive sexual approaches by An-An, she is not prepared to mate with him.'

The optimism that prevailed during the early stage of the project, they explained, was due to the feeling that it was Chi-Chi's fear of the male that was suppressing her sexual responses, but this proved to be not the case:

'Even after her fear had subsided she was still not prepared to mate with him, and in a preference situation chose to offer herself sexually to a human observer rather than to the male panda.'

The report concluded with the comment that:
'Hopes for a normal mating are slender,' but it emphasised, 'they *cannot be ruled out entirely.*'

I personally was one of those who felt that the subsequent attempt in London was well worth a try.

Considering the fact that Chi-Chi and An-An were – and still are – the only two captive giant pandas in the West – a successful mating could have been of tremendous im-

First Catch Your Tiger

portance in the zoological field. Now that the experiment has failed, its implications have been spelled out very clearly by three men closely associated with the later project in London: Dr M. R. Brambell, Dr J. W. Rowlands and Mr I. M. Hime, and I feel that this account of the Chi-Chi and An-An affair would be incomplete without at least a partial quotation of their views.

Writing in *Nature** they have since recalled that:

'Since 1936, when the first live giant panda was taken from China to the United States, there have been seventeen of these animals in Western zoos: only two survive, Moscow's male An-An and London's female Chi-Chi, both aged about 12. The greatest longevity so far recorded is 14 years 8 months. Until now, there has only been one true pair living together as adults outside China and North Korea, where at least two have been bred in captivity. St Louis Zoo kept a pair together from 1939 to 1946 which must have become adult, but there were no reports of mating and breeding.'

After reviewing the failures of the efforts to mate An-An and Chi-Chi, which the writers, while agreeing that 'maybe one or both of the animals no longer recognise giant pandas as their own kind,' say the cause is 'impossible to pinpoint', the article concludes with these thoughts of the future:

'For giant pandas to remain a viable species they must be bred in captivity. They require large areas of land in the wild and it may not be practicable to ensure their survival merely by protecting the natural habitat. The fact that our efforts have been restricted to two animals does not lessen their significance. It merely makes it more difficult to use controlled observations to test the important factors. Had we found how to make these two animals breed, we might have carried into another generation our investigations into the management of giant pandas. We must now

* June 21st, 1969.

Zoo-Men's Dilemma

hope that the zoologists of Peking can carry on with their successes and that enough giant pandas can be bred in captivity to ensure survival of the species.'

*

An over-identification with man? The advance of old age? Or factors that, maybe, are peculiar to a species of which we know comparatively little? The pandas breeding habits are still largely a mystery.

Of specially violent cases of rape or sexual assault it is often said that the guilty male had 'behaved like an animal'. In actual fact, an animal's sexual reactions to given circumstances are often less predictable – and more 'civilised' – than man's. In some cases, the sex itself is more difficult to define. Thus although it took years to confirm that Chi-Chi was really female, our panda was not unique in that respect.

At one time the Zoo was extremely proud of having acquired two very fine specimens – male and female – of the rare maned wolf; a diminishing species. But all efforts to induce the twain to breed were unrewarded, and in our wisdom we argued reasons as to why this should be so.

We had long been perplexed by the failure of captive lionesses – held not only in Regent's Park but in other zoos as well – to conceive, and were only gradually realising that this was due in part to war-time deficiencies of diet among the specimens from which we re-stocked when the war was over. But the failure of the long-maned wolves we traced to a less sophisticated source – they never seemed to want to copulate.

Contrary to the beliefs of many a 'superior' human, animals are often shy in their sexual activities and will react adversely if they are aware of being observed. So, except in rare circumstances, and then only when it was possible to

First Catch Your Tiger

camouflage our surveillance, it was our policy to leave them very much on their own.

It was obvious, however, that something more than 'shyness' was responsible for the wolves undue disinterest in each other; and eventually we resigned ourselves to the rather rueful thought that this could only be explained by the Zoo's having made an unlucky bargain. With *neither* member of the pair showing the will to mate, their purchase was, to say the least, unfortunate.

It was only when the outcome of a savage, undignified, fracas brought the female into the Zoo hospital that we discovered the real reason for the wolf's lack of sexual response. The occasion arose from a dispute over whose food was whose – the Number One cause of conflict among our captive animals – and the male emerged the winner, fracturing his 'mate's' leg. This made it necessary to operate immediately and we resorted to use of intramedullary pinning to secure the fractured bone in postion. The operation was entirely successful, and soon our patient was out in the sun again, and exercising in its den.

Considering the fact that the animal's life had been in danger, for the thin, rather brittle, legs of the maned wolf are not the easiest of limbs for surgery, this was in itself extremely gratifying – but a less talked-about aspect of the operation was the fact that it led to the sex of the 'female' being re-classified. On the operating table we had discovered that the Zoo's reluctant breeders were both males!

*

So far unsubsidised by the State, and reliant for its very existence on the fees paid by its visitors and the gifts of private patronage, London Zoo is unique as regards the way in which it seeks to provide a full range of scientific, educa-

Zoo-Men's Dilemma

tional, breeding and animal medical services. It is also unique for the manner in which – as exemplified in the case of the pandas – it involves itself in international projects of wide-ranging importance even when obliged to effect the most stringent economies in the administration of its everyday affairs.

However, there are times when the very scope of its ambitions, however praiseworthy, may give rise to concern about their practicability, or indeed the order of priorities involved.

The celebrated aviary, for example, hailed though it has been as an 'adventure' in architecture, has worried some well-wishers of the Zoo. Perturbed by reports that it has cost £120,000 – or twice the total expended on the hospital – they feel that the price is high for housing, at the most, some 200 birds. Similar criticism has been levelled at the Elephant Pavilion. Costing £250,000 this edifice is admittedly eye-catching – though described by one unkind cynic as 'emotive of elephants' bottoms' – when designed it lacked such practicable facilities as sky-hooks, to lift its giant inmates should they fall.

Built in times of financial stringency, other costly projects were the result of private bounty, but some observers feel that part at least of the funds donated for them could have been employed in areas less prestigious but liable to benefit a wider range of animals.

The unexampled diversity of the Zoo's activities – often regarded as its crowning glory – has also caused some confusion of opinion, and at times has tended to divide its closest supporters. To a large extent this is an inevitable development for – as is the case with a major political party – the Zoo appeals to its followers for a variety of reasons, and not *all* of these are reasons held in common.

First Catch Your Tiger

Entertaining enthusiasm for one shade of the spectrum, some zoophiles are not necessarily enchanted by the regard shown by their colleagues for the others.

One celebrated example of this division of opinion as to what is desirable as a Zoo activity, and what is not, directly involved myself and the hospital staff. At issue was a programme of research and experiment, including investigation into the field of transplant surgery.

16. Extramural Activities

By the early 'sixties, it had become obvious from the pages of the press – both medical and lay – that the transplant era was upon us, and that in America, in particular, surgical teams were already engaged in extensive homotransplant (man to man) experiments.

There were also moves in the field of heterotransplantation namely the transfer of organs from animals of differing species but of similar genes, and already we had heard of people in renal failure whose lives had been salvaged for the time being by the advantageous use of kidneys taken from chimpanzees.

During a visit to America, I was most impressed at the progress of this work, its scope epitomised by one well-known researcher, who revealed to me that he had no fewer than ninety chimpanzees available for kidney transplants.

The chimps were housed in three different centres, and the details of their white cells had been computerised and stored. The idea was that when a suitable patient urgently needed a kidney replacement that could not be obtained from man, *his* computerised data was compared by yet another computer, which selected the chimp best suited for a transplant.

Justifiably, the researcher concerned was proud of his organisation in general, but especially was he proud of the fact that he could have a chimp flown in from any one of the centres, and made available for an operation in any part of the country in a matter of hours.

There were also experiments under way in the use of the kidneys of baboons, 'tissue-typed' in a similar way to the chimpanzees, but these were as yet on a very minor scale.

Personally, I found this line of investigation quite fascinating and full of exciting implications for people whose lives would otherwise be impossible to save, and I was thus most interested to discover that similar experiments were being conducted in Britain. However, at that time, my interest was purely academic, and I had no idea that it was soon to be extended into practice.

This was partly as a result of two remarkable institutions being established within the boundaries of the Zoo, the Nuffield Institute of Comparative Medicine and the Wellcome Institute of Comparative Physiology.

*

The casual visitor to the Zoological Gardens may be forgiven for assuming that all of the buildings he sees there are of the Zoo, Zoological! But this is not so. Comparatively new arrivals, the Nuffield Institute and the Wellcome Institute are integral parts of the Zoo and the work they do is arranged and approved by advisory committees.

They contribute to a greater knowledge of the management, nutrition and needs of zoo animals. They also yield knowledge which is of use to the health and disease of man and animal.

The Nuffield Institute, established with the aid of £140,000 of Nuffield money, first settled in the Gardens in 1964, with its objective the comparative medicine of disease and other factors common to both man and animals.

Extramural Activities

Some of the Nuffield's study is directed towards the problems of infection, and the problems of nutrition, but few projects of science remain in isolation for long, and the flow and interflow of information throws tributaries into areas far-removed from those originally defined.

Thus it was not long before the researchers of the institutions were drawing on the experience provided by the veterinary service, and in some respects their investigations began greatly to assist our own.

Possessing its own set of skills and standards, and with its own varying types of equipment and techniques, each had something valuable to offer to the other, and the collaboration between us soon developed to a state where our efforts were more or less integrated.

It was as a result of this working partnership, and my known interest in the transplant revolution, that I found myself in close contact with Mr X, a brilliant young surgeon whose ambitions lay beyond the horizon of our immediate programme, and were to result in his later becoming the leader of a prominent British transplant team, of international repute.

X asked if I would help him in an investigational project designed to examine the potential of the baboon as a renal transplant donor, and this proved to be a fairly heavy commitment.

Heavy because until you witness it and indeed take part in it, it is quite impossible to appreciate the depth of thought and planning that research workers in general dedicate to their programmes. To them, time is quite meaningless—they may well start their research surgery at 8 a.m. or 8 p.m. depending on their commitments, and they will work unceasingly for hours to perfect their art and science.

First Catch Your Tiger

I began to appreciate this when Mr. X gave me this chance to join his team—although in a small and minor way. His task was to investigate the potential of large baboons as possible donors of organs, a matter which had already received some attention in America and South Africa apart from other places. One of the major problems facing the team was how to manage the restraint, sedation and anaesthesia of the huge, fearsome adult male animals which proved so suitable a size for surgery. It was felt that I could help, and indeed the problems of the approach to the baboons were precisely the same that had been faced and, through necessity, overcome in the earlier days of the Zoo Hospital.

Thus I joined this exciting and forward-looking team of people working in a research institute some distance from the Zoo, and the experience was quite fascinating.

It has always been so very exciting and indeed enlightening for me to know just how willing my medical colleagues are to involve veterinary surgeons in their programmes concerning animals. Clearly, each has something to offer the other, and both learn tremendously. Many medical researchers believe that a veterinary surgeon should always be involved where their experiments involve animals, but naturally a special sort of training and expertise is expected from the veterinary surgeon which differs from that required, say, for the farmyard or drawing-room.

My own interest in, and enthusiasm for, comparative medicine as a rewarding field of endeavour only increases with the passing of time; for so long all disciplines within the discipline of Medicine have tended to 'go it alone.' Modern technology and the pace of science today have re-emphasised the fact that not only the tycoon individual surgeon is a thing of the past now that team work is so

Extramural Activities

essential, but the intermingling of disciplines has become as essential within a team as the multiplicity of experts. No one person can cope any more with all the details he attempted to do in the past—the very depth and spread of modern knowledge has made this impossible. The march of science in last decade—never mind the last 100 years—has been both so remarkable and formidable that it has perhaps even outstripped man's ability to comprehend it. For example—the modern operating theatre may have so many electronic devices within it that it looks like the command module of a spaceship and demands science graduates to control it. No wonder a team is needed. No wonder we feel awed by it all while watching men walking on the moon.

But to be more earthy for a moment, the team I had been invited to join had had in mind the baboon as a potential kidney donor to a doomed man for whom no alternative was available. However, death overtook him so swiftly that nothing further was done.

*

As subsequent events in the career of transplant surgery were all too clearly to show, it is doubtful whether our intervention, even had we been able to make it in time, could have done anything to have saved the man. But this we were not to know, and we regarded the event as a tragic disappointment, made the more so by the fact that such opportunities to save life (as we saw it) might not come again. Difficulties were arising in the climate of the Society's activities in the realms of scientific experiment, and prominent in effecting this climatic disturbance was the redoubtable Lady Dowding.

Originally, this very charming and very determined lady, who showed almost as much tenacity in combating anything that she considered to be cruelty to animals as her husband displayed against the Luftwaffe during the Battle of Britain, had joined the Society with the intention of 'helping' Guy, the Zoo's giant gorilla.

Guy, she felt, was in 'a very tragic state' for lack of companionship. But what seemed to have evaded Lady Dowding's attention was the fact that failure to provide the gorilla with a mate was not due to negligence, but to acute concern. Perhaps to an even greater extent than Chi-Chi, Guy was orientated towards man. He might not appreciate a female in his den – but time will tell.

Later, however, Lady Dowding widened her range of interests to include other aspects of zoo life, and in one of these her intervention had positive consequences.

The first indications of trouble to come arose when there was a request for information about rumours that 'surgical experiments' were being conducted on Zoo premises.

But, be that as it may, Lady Dowding's move certainly had repercussions, and particularly on a clinical programme we had instituted in the Hospital, where we were still investigating the low fertility of Zoo lionesses, a considerable cause of concern to zoo-keepers throughout the country, and dating back to the post-war re-stocking.

Our plans entailed ovulating our patients by injecting them with hormones, subsequently resorting to surgery by opening their abdomens for internal examination to check the ovary for results. Was this programme, we wondered, to be completely set at hazard?

I had defined the work involved simply as being 'clinical investigation', but to others, I now realised, it might appear to be otherwise. Reluctantly, I decided that I must shelve the project until I could get a ruling.

Extramural Activities

In the meantime, and as part of a developing field of activity which I shall so much enjoy, I was privileged to assist a team of surgeons based a good few miles out of London in a project which was designed to explore the rejection phenomena as it applied to heterotransplantation of organs – in this case, again kidneys. The team were taking kidneys from purchased dingoes and putting them into research beagles to check if and when and how soon rejection processes would begin. Man would be the poorer without the dedication and precision of these men whose care for their own patients is reflected in the care they show over their experimental animals.

Predictably, the arrangement whereby the practices of the research institutions, housed in quarters within the Zoo, were free of the restrictions imposed on the Zoo itself, did not pass unnoticed by the anti-vivisectionist lobby. Nor were they permitted to proceed without a protest.

I quote without comment *The Times* report of an event that, at the time, occasioned me considerable personal regret:

'Lady Dowding, chairman of the National Anti-Vivisection Society, has resigned as a fellow of the Zoological Society of London because, she says, a laboratory licensed by the Home Office to conduct experiments on animals is being built in the Zoo grounds ...

'At a press conference yesterday, Lady Dowding said that she had written to Sir Solly Zuckerman, secretary of the Zoological Society, seeking information about the laboratory. She had been told in reply that no animals in the Zoo's collection were to be used for experiments, but that a licence had been obtained under the Cruelty to Animals Act.

'She had surmised that the Zoo would get domestic animals from dealers, and laboratory animals for experiments. "I have resigned because I regard the Zoo as a sanctuary for animals, and now they have built a laboratory there", she said. "I would never belong to a society engaged in experiments on animals."'

The Zoological Society's reaction to this statement was also quoted in *The Times* report. 'We have no comment on Lady Dowding's resignation,' said a spokesman. 'We wish however to make it quite clear that no experiments have been, or will be, made on animals in our collection.'

*

My involvement in the transplant field came to an end when X left London and moved on – to conduct more complex researches, and, in so doing, to achieve great things.

Also at an end was our participation in another little-known and 'politically controversial' line of research; one that may yet have great signification in the realm of conservation.

Together with a keen Ph.D. I had been working on the application of A.I. (artificial insemination) as a means of solving the breeding problems of animals in captivity and re-stocking species that were becoming progressively more rare.

Our first major venture into what was then a field of science hitherto restricted to the domestic animal or man, involved a male Arabian oryx, a member of the antelope family that, plentiful until a decade or so earlier, had fallen victim to the vast increase in fire-power possessed by the sporting inhabitants of the Arabian peninsula.

To the sheiks and their followers, the oryx was not only a source of food: it was also a status symbol with phallic implications. To kill one was an assertion of the hunter's masculinity, and in this respect even the machine-gun was enlisted as an ally.

As a result of this combination of superstition and modern

Extramural Activities

hardware the toll among the handsome animals was heavy, and continued to be so until it was suddenly – but very belatedly – realised that the oryx had become almost extinct.

When we first commenced our collaboration, the application of A.I. to creatures of the wild was almost unknown, but my colleague aimed to perfect the practice and extend it in a very big way indeed. It should be possible, he thought, to extract the sperm from male wild animals to service females not only in zoos in Britain but also in those overseas.

He argued that methods should be devised of storing the sperm, just as the blood for blood transfusions was stored, and sperm banks should be established, for use on a worldwide basis. Among other things this would obviate the stresses inherent on animals being forced to travel long distances to service – or be serviced by – mates they had not seen before, in an alien environment.

To most of us, the desirability of this ambitious scheme was obvious enough, but how could it be achieved? All operations involving wild animals were beset by obvious difficulties, but the procedure required for semen extraction promised to pose problems all of its own. Compared with, say, a tiger, or the highly nervous gazelle, even the most ferocious bull would be easy to deal with.

It was not until much thought – and not a little discussion had occured, that we agreed a technique that was comparatively simple, and well-known in farm animals.

First, a Cap-chur dart containing sedative was fired into the animal's rump, to introduce a degree of sedation. And then, once the animal had been anaesthetised, we introduced into its rectum an electrical device which stimulated its sexual reactions, bringing about ejaculation.

It will be recalled that, on the inception of the abortive

First Catch Your Tiger

Chi-Chi and An-An affair, we suggested to the Russians that A.I. might be a more effective method of breeding than 'putting together' animals that were complete strangers to each other, and one of which at least was heavily 'imprinted' by man.

At the time, our suggestion was rejected, and probably for good reason: but looking to the future, and the improvement in insemination techniques and sperm storage that are bound to come about as the result of further research, it is exciting to think of what A.I. can mean in terms of the conservation of rare species.

On cost grounds alone, its advantages are tremendous, by eliminating the expense of elaborate transport and escort facilities for animals being moved from one country, or continent, to another. But the chances A.I. will offer for the improvement of stock are even more impressive, whatever problems it may seem to pose, in the short-term, to traditionalist ideas of breeding.

Beyond my task at the Zoo, I held an appointment with a research unit where animals cartilage transplants were conducted, using sheep as donors, to help investigate the cause of arthritis in man, and work towards a cure. Prosthetic implants were carried out on goats, to facilitate the design of artificial joints and limbs for human patients. And we also used goats as 'models' for artificial hip joints.

The reason for this latter move was that the goat has long legs, and as he must be able to use his artificial hip the moment he comes out of anaesthesia, any error in design is quickly identified.

One early experiment in this direction ended in failure. During the months after operation, the ball of the newly-fitted hip penetrated its pelvis, and we had painlessly to destroy it. The hip had been made *too* well, as a perfect fit. No one had thought that you don't have a perfectly spherical hip, any more than you have perfectly balanced teeth.

While opposed to every form of cruelty towards animals, it was – and still is – a source of surprise to me, that there should be such opposition to experiments on animals when the only valid alternative is to experiment on humans, or else to impose a standstill on many forms of medical progress that could be applied to relieve the suffering of both animals and people.

Similar considerations surely must apply to the question of testing artificial limbs of unknown viability. To expose an animal to risk is a distinctly unpleasant thing to have to do – but what is the alternative? Should one test out the untried appliance on one's wife? Or dispense with the limbs altogether? No, if such a question of choice arises, and always provided we ensure that the animal is used wisely and humanely, there is no doubt in the researcher's mind as to what that choice must be.

The cross-pollination of ideas arising from the close relationship between the Zoo scientific staff and the staffs of other institutions, had an effect that was most stimulating and constructive.

*

Many zoologists admit that there is today a crisis of thinking concerning zoos and their purpose, and some of them claim that it is very much overdue.

Despite the educational advantages derived from zoo-visiting – its scope epitomised by the annual pilgrimage of schoolchildren to Regent's Park – it is pompous to suggest, as some do, that a zoo's purpose is primarily an educational

First Catch Your Tiger

one. Education *is* a benefit, but in many zoos it is a fringe benefit only. Who bothers to assimilate the informative notes attached to a tiger's cage? Who derives any lasting value from perusing the Latin title of, say, the boas and pythons (the family *Bosidae*)? How many visitors really care about the genera of the order *Crocodilia*?

While it may be said that it educates us, intrigues or stimulates us, a zoo – *any* zoo – first indulges our idle curiosity and gratifies our ego. The monkey house puts on show a parody of our manners, but it is a parody that serves to flatter, not annoy. From participating in 'tea parties', to dressing, or undressing themselves, the apes can only mimic what we do naturally, and the conceit of homo sapiens is enhanced by the comparison.

In 1964, I told the U.F.A.W. Summer Congress: 'There is no comprehending man's supreme egotism when he relates his presence at the top of the evolutionary peak to his own skill in getting there, and couples this with a pitying observation of all the other animals who have not.'

I have since had no reason to modify this view. The zoo is a wonderful place for compounding one's own satisfaction with oneself by contemplating and pitying – perhaps subconsciously – others less well endowed with facilities for advancement.

Among some zoologists and conservationists – and some zoo directors too – there is a feeling that there is something not quite wholesome about the type of attraction that zoos exert today.

This belief springs from considerations that are both complex and divergent, and reflects a cleavage of opinion in the ranks of zoo people – hitherto solid – that may yet give rise to a philosophy on zoo-keeping. This philosophy is urgently required.

Extramural Activities

Contrary to what may be popularly imagined, the dialogue now in progress has little directly to do with the morality of placing animals in captivity. There is nothing that is 'cruel' in the physical sense of the word, about a system that ensures for an animal, normally exposed to the hazards of survival in the jungle or the bush, the provision of food, shelter, and medical care. The current dialogue questions instead the very *raison d'être* of zoos as we know them today. Are they to continue to be akin to glorified stamp collections? Are their directors always to have the aim before them of collecting one at least of every specimen in the hope that some of those specimens may be precious or rare? Or should there be an alternative objective?

By certain persons of influence, their efforts not the less highly regarded for being restricted to fund-raising, the undoubted need of our zoos for increased custom has led to their being projected as types of living museums, where the exhibits walk, eat and even beg – do parlour tricks and are bred – for the amusement of the visitor, and the visitor alone. Just what are we to think of this type of exhibition? And, if we don't like it, what shall we put in its place?

Some years ago, in the course of a magazine article on zoos and their purpose, I wrote:

'Like many other collective nouns, "zoo" is used to describe any collection of unusual animals not normally seen living naturally or domestically in the area where the zoo is established. Where this collection of animals is, as it were, put to work as a form of entertainment, the zoo may then become a circus. This activity is an extension of the one where wild animals are made captive for exhibition, and involves the animals in training and performance of acts which some regard as unnecessary, if not undignified. I think we must keep clear in our minds the

First Catch Your Tiger

fact that this extension is a separate issue . . . some believe that this distinction between the zoo proper and the circus today is becoming rather too blurred for comfort.'

Educational . . . conservational . . . a medium of entertainment, or a laboratory in which to study comparative medicine . . . certainly there is no shortage of ideas as to what a zoo's purpose should be, but most of those ideas are poles apart from each other.

In the ranks of the conservationists there are certain visionaries – my friend Gerald Durrell among them – who look to A.I. as a means of enabling the zoos to act as major begetters of life, breeding where considered desirable, whole colonies of species decimated by man (who then piously declares them in danger of extinction!). And there are others to whom, as we have seen, this ideal is almost anathema.

There is also the school that would use the major zoos as convenient collecting-grounds for animals that could then be used for a wide variety of scientific purposes, including exploration of the complex pattern of evolution.

But, shadowing every one of these ideas – however controversial – is the question of finance. When all is said and done, the manager of commercial zoos has to make a profit. To purchase new animals, and care for their health and welfare; to build suitable accommodation for those animals and cover the overheads of the place in which they are shown . . . such necessities can only be provided from a zoo's profits, and those profits will largely depend on the attractions the place has to offer.

The scientific activities of the major British zoos are acclaimed by sympathetic observers as being based on the highest principles, and possessing great implications for the future. But the fact of the matter is that such activities

Extramural Activities

mean little to the zoos in terms of their life-blood – money. And to expedite them may well demand expenditures unlikely to be met from income without serious impact on profit margins. The scientific institutes at London Zoo happily attract grants from funding organizations in a way which other zoos may well envy, not to mention a recent Government grant of £1.6 million.

Thus, in the ultimate, zoos may even have to ponder the morality of their financing scientific projects – or projects in respect of zoo architecture and so forth – out of funds provided by the visiting public, or indeed any other source which believes its contributions are being used exclusively for the maintenance of animals and staff.

But then what happens? Do we revert to the other extreme? Bring all progress to a stop, and practise pinchbeck economies? Rely on the technique of the fairground barker to bring in the crowds, and the gate-money? Present to an ever more critical and discerning public a brand-image for an inferior type of product? Few serious observers would like to contemplate such an apparent perversion of established standards.

Many zoos – particularly British zoos – are today financially at the cross-roads. Confronted by so many competing forms of entertainment, they have failed to maintain in *real terms* an income equivalent to that which they realised in the immediate post-war heyday. Nor should there be any great mystery about this, even though some would keep it so. The prices demanded for animals are fantastically high, overheads and staff costs have soared, fiscal measures imposed by the Government have dampened generous giving.

The financial predicament created by this cycle is particularly noticeable in the case of many fly-by-night holiday resort zoos that now find themselves able to survive only by

First Catch Your Tiger

buying-in exhibits at the beginning of the season, and selling them at its end. Mercifully, there is now an organisation in Britain* that exists to raise and maintain zoo standards, and it is to be hoped that local authorities will follow its advice, and help uphold the code that it establishes. But London Zoo has problems of a more complicated kind.

With so much expenditure devoted to maintaining its prestige, and the furtherance of its pioneering tradition, London Zoo has problems that are commensurate to its size. Indeed, it is even possible to contemplate the possibility that London – or indeed any other zoo with a similar sense of mission – may eventually run into such difficulties that the Government of the day may be forced to consider financial assistance.

Should this occur, then those problems that have hitherto been met by the donations of individual millionaires, would be placed in the Government's own court, and receive governmental solutions. But do we really want this situation to arise? Is it in fact at all likely to arise?

From my own observations, in a purely veterinary capacity, I have noted the price of vital medical equipment creep steadily upwards, and have seen the cost of replacing dead animals escalate beyond all estimates. They still continue to do so, while income in real terms, falls. Can London Zoo, or other big British zoos, continue to pursue their programmes – independent of Government or civic subsidy? Can it continue to rely on private philanthropy, in face of fiscal restrictions and adverse trends in popular taste?

Before we can get an answer to such questions, it is essential for a dialogue to be established – and fairly quickly – as to what we expect from our zoos, and what we are prepared to give.

* The Federation of British Zoos

Exodus

No other silence is quite like that of the Zoo at night. It is a thick silence, brooding and oppressive, and at the same time it is wakeful – pregnant with apprehension.

It follows the phenomenon that Zoo people call 'The Roar-Off' – that nightly outcry from the creatures within its boundaries to which every species makes its own peculiar contribution. The hoarse bark of the seal, the *basso profundo* of the lion, the tapering howl of the jackals, housed near the camel house – for five minutes, and always around ten o'clock, Regent's Park gives vent to the cries of the captive wild: then the silence falls like a well-stuffed pillow, smothering all.

Only when the watchman goes on his rounds is there any deviation from this almost audible hush. A screech from the peafowl means he is passing the pools; the hoot of an owl equates with his reaching the North Aviary; a formless chatter, delivered at high speed, presages his appearance by the Monkey House: you can trace the watchman's every move by the type of sound that greets it. But such alarums are momentary in their impact, and make no lasting impression on the silence. Soon it has re-asserted its heavy sway: a silence that can be heard, like the surge of the 'sea' in a shell.

Leave the hospital behind you, and enter the Gardens on foot, and the slumber of the place seems as absolute as the darkness, Africa-black. But go on patrol in your car, and

First Catch Your Tiger

switch on the headlights, and a thousand wakeful eyes, until then unseen, will glitter bright as stars before slipping into shy and immediate eclipse. The Zoo silence is the silence imposed by primeval fear: the dread of the approaching predator. Beneath it lurks an omnipresent sense of menace...

It is intriguing to ponder what might happen if some form of revealing light were to be thrown, not at animals in their cages, but on the structure and financing of the zoo as it exists today. What fears would be revealed beneath its impressive surface, the outward assurance of the world's biggest living museum? What doubts would be exposed regarding the future of the most varied animal collection to have been gathered together in one place since time began? Is there perhaps a way in which those fears may be allayed? A way in which, while still satisfying their educational, scientific and conservationist roles, the major zoos may retain (or regain) their status of crowd-pullers, and maintain financial viability in the bargain?

In a thoughtful contribution to the debate that is now being conducted over the whole philosophy of zoo-keeping, Desmond Morris recently hit back at those who argue that because of such comparatively new developments as the animal safari (for those who can afford it) and the T.V. screen (for those who can't) zoos in general are now redundant, and should be abolished.

'I for one,' he says, 'can not say Death to the Zoo, I remember to this day my first visit to one, a visit that did more for my later interest in animals than a hundred films or a thousand books. The animals were real, and they were near, and they got through to me.'

Morris argues that, without zoos, our vast urban population will become so physically remote from animal life that they will cease to care about it. 'Eventually someone will find the animal equivalent of the plastic flower, and that will be that!'

However, the purely traditional type of institution, 'where the design of the cage is shrunk and the design becomes uniform in the interests of economy', receives no support from his controversial pen. 'Dens where, in the name of hygiene, living conditions are reduced to a sterile minimum, with perches, tiles and slabs of concrete being utilised in place of messy leaves, branches, rocks and earth,' have no place in his scheme of things.

Instead, he would like to seek premises 'where animals can fulfil their real behaviour patterns, and be seen to do so.' And as few present-day zoos could be adapted to such a purpose he sees the solution lying in the specialised zoo, which would cater 'not for the highly specific demands of 500 widely differing species, but say for one group of closely related species.' A new level of zoo-keeping, with carefully controlled breeding units would result from such an arrangement or so he feels. Above all, the animals would be fun to watch, and very instructive too.

Should Morris's idea of a zoo be adopted he promises us a sensationally new kind of animal spectacle ('imagine 30 African elephants on a miniature African plain'). Elephants, rhinos, and hippos would be seen, 'in their natural groups, wallowing in artificial rivers and mud baths.'

An exciting prospect? A vista of challenge and opportunity combined? Without necessarily sharing all my colleague's views on such topics as the 'immorality' of imposing cage-life on an animal, there is no doubt that what he is advocating is, in this instance, both interesting and valuable, and expressive of a school of thought that is receiving increasing attention and support.

First Catch Your Tiger

In the past, and in the present too, the major zoos were housed in the midst of the major cities. This siting was dictated by practical necessity, namely the need for the zoos to be accessible to the maximum number of people. Now, in the era of the car and motorway, it seems logical to suppose that our animal collections need no longer be confined to the big population centres, but can be transferred to sites deep in the countryside.

Animals are infinitely fascinating when you are able to see them in their natural habitat, and a progressive policy of evacuation for the larger species would leave metropolitan zoos responsible for catering for animals less well suited to the rigour of existence in the country, and these could then be exhibited in surroundings that would enable them to give their personal traits full play.

Will this sort of arrangement – attractive to both the animal and the visitor – provide the basic pattern for the zoos of the future? Or will some other form of exhibition take its place?

Whatever the answer, it is certain that the world's zoophiles will want to see their zoos as live and healthy organisations, of benefit to animals and man. They will be sorry indeed should financial illness turn into a killing disease, and, just as they expect their veterinary service to act decisively when treating an ailing animal, so will they expect a similar decisiveness on the part of the zoo authorities, when confronted by disturbing symptoms in the zoos themselves, symptoms that are now becoming apparent.

In the case of a patient in the Zoo Hospital, sharp surgery is employed only as the very last resort, but often it is the only effective one. The time comes when temporary palliatives, however ingenious, cease to soothe, and only the knife can save. In the broader context that involves, not only the fate of the individual animal but the health of the zoos themselves, there are some who feel that the need for surgery may be approaching faster than we think.